J SHEEKEY FISH

Published by Preface 2012

10 9 8 7 6 5 4 3 2

First published in Great Britain in 2012 by Preface Publishing

20 Vauxhall Bridge Road
London, SW1V 2SA

An imprint of The Random House Group Limited

www.randomhouse.co.uk
www.prefacepublishing.co.uk

Addresses for companies within The Random House Group Limited
can be found at www.randomhouse.co.uk

The Random House Group Limited Reg. No. 954009

A CIP catalogue record for this book is available from the British Library

ISBN 978 1 84809 380 5

The Random House Group Limited supports The Forest Stewardship
Council (FSC®), the leading international forest certification organisation.
Our books carrying the FSC label are printed on FSC® certified paper. FSC is
the only forest certification scheme endorsed by the leading environmental
organisations, including Greenpeace. Our paper procurement policy can be
found at www.randomhouse.co.uk/environment

Designed by Two Associates
Printed and bound in Italy by Graphicom srl

J SHEEKEY FISH

WRITER ALLAN JENKINS
CHEF TIM HUGHES
PHOTOGRAPHY HOWARD SOOLEY

preface

CONTENTS

J SHEEKEY

CENTRAL LONDON, WINTER MORNING, 7AM STILL DARK. Theatreland's lights are dimmed, actors and audiences left hours ago, the only people moving are an occasional policeman and the J Sheekey chefs waiting for deliveries from the many corners of Britain's coastline.

First, wooden crates of native oysters that have been arriving at our door for more than a century. Gathered on the Essex coast since even before the Roman garrisons, today's are packed 100 to a box, cup-side down and covered with cooling seaweed. We will sell 300 to 400 today in half dozens and dozens, delicately poached in watercress soup or as the centrepiece to fruits de mer.

Next to arrive, shellfish harvested in the icy waters off the Isle of Mull: langoustines caught in creels unchanged for centuries. Scallops hand-gathered only the day before off the sea bed, to be served simply roasted in the shell. More deliveries come quickly: a box of beautiful turbot, the king of fish, and our signature Dover sole to be cooked whole on the bone and filleted with spoons, just as J Sheekey cooks have done for more than 100 years. Cornish cod arrives next, smelling sweetly of the sea, jewel-like musky red mullet, tentacled squid fished from Channel waters. Downstairs, chefs are skinning, pin-boning, trimming fins, portioning fish, making stocks, stacking the fridges with freshly caught slip soles, pollack, photogenic John Dory, each cook moving almost invisibly, fluidly in the narrow spaces.

Outside, there are many more people now, in buses, cars; commuters are walking up Charing Cross Road on their way to work. Some will pop in later for a fish pie for lunch. Others will come for a cocktail before seeing a play at one of the many theatres that surround this area of the West End. There will be couples, families, friends coming to celebrate a birthday or anniversary. Others just seeking a great fish supper. Post-theatre, there will be late workers, actors and their audiences, looking to unwind from the night's performance in an understated ambience of impeccable service.

Then, just a few hours later, after the restaurant is cleared and cleaned and the cooks have taken the night bus home, more crates of oysters will arrive, more chefs, more fish, for another day and another showing of the longest running theatreland performance in London.

ROBERT ARTHUR TALBOT GASCOYNE-CECIL, 3rd Marquess of Salisbury, is best remembered by historians for the Boer War, the Anglo-Japanese Treaty and for three terms as Prime Minister of Britain during the late Victorian era. But food lovers have another reason to remember – and thank – him: for his patronage of Josef Sheekey, a fish and oyster trader in Shepherd's Market, Mayfair.

It was while serving his last term in office, in 1896, that Salisbury granted Josef premises in St Martin's Court to serve poached and steamed fish, seafood and shellfish, with the proviso he also supply meals to the Prime Minister's famous after-theatre dinner parties. The restaurant soon became popular with leading theatrical personalities, agents and promoters of the day, while still attracting the traders of Covent Garden Market.

Its glorious heyday came during the 1950s and '60s under the ownership of Josef's formidable granddaughter, the legendary Mrs Williams, whose portrait is still on our walls. Under subsequent ownership it slowly declined, until in 1998, it was bought by Chris Corbin and Jeremy King, who had an ambition to add a classic British fish and seafood restaurant to their Le Caprice and Ivy stable.

Corbin and King retained renowned designer David Collins with a brief to create a new restaurant that evoked the best of the old. The signature portraits of theatrical luminaries who had patronised the restaurant were lovingly re-framed and hung with an obsessive eye for detail that caused many of King's friends to despair.

Period paintings were chosen with the help of surrealist expert and jazz singer George Melly and art historian Richard Shone. The menu remained faithful to the spirit of the original, too, although the 3rd Marquess's stipulation against fried fish was relaxed a little to allow room for our famous fish and chips.

J Sheekey quietly re-opened its doors on Friday, 6 November 1998 to acclaim from critics and old customers. Theatrical regulars returned, including Cate Blanchett, Helen Mirren and Alan Rickman, who favoured Champagne with chips. London's best-loved fish and seafood restaurant had effortlessly returned to its glamorous glory.

In 2005 the restaurant passed into the sure hands of Richard Caring, who added our sister fish restaurant Scott's in Mayfair. And, finally, when the space next door to J Sheekey became available, the art deco Oyster Bar was born, with a new series of contemporary theatrical portraits commissioned. With its concentration on serving classic seafood and shellfish, perhaps half a dozen natives with Champagne, we like to think that, after 116 years, the old Marquess and Josef Sheekey would approve.

FISH CHART

Brill

Scophthalmus rhombus

Brown shrimp

Crangon crangon

Clam

Mercenaria mercenaria

Cockle

Cerastoderma edule

Cod

Gadus morhua

Crab

Cancer pagurus

Dover sole

Solea solea

Dublin Bay prawn

Nephrops norvegicus

Gurnard

Chelidonichthys cuculus

Haddock

Melanogrammus aeglefinus

Hake

Merluccius merluccius

Halibut

Hippoglossus hippoglossus

Herring

Clupea harengus

John Dory

Zeus faber

Lemon sole

Microstomus kitt

Lobster (native)

Homarus gammarus

Mackerel

Scomber scombrus

Monkfish

Lophius piscatorius

Mussels

Mytilus edulis

Oyster (native)
Ostrea edulis

Oyster (rock)
Crassostrea gigas

Plaice
Pleuronectes platessa

Pollack
Pollachius pollachius

Razor clam
Ensis directus

Red mullet
Mullus barbatus

Sardine
Sardina pilchardus

Scallop
Pectinidae

Sea bass
Dicentrarchus labrax

Sea bream
Sparus aurata

Sea trout
Salmo trutta

Squid
Loligo vulgaris

Tiger prawn
Penaeus monodon

Turbot
Psetta maxima

Whelk
Buccinum undatum

Whitebait
Spratus spratus

Wild salmon
Salmo salar

Winkle
Littorina littorea

WHEN FISH IS THE HERO

COOKING FISH IS ABOUT CONFIDENCE, a good non-stick pan and an efficient hot grill. There is no need to be nervous. The first and most important thing is to find a good supplier. Track down a fishmonger you can trust – travel if you have to – because at the moment they are more under threat than some fish. Support them, make friends with them. If you have a good relationship with your fishmonger, he or she will be happy to supply you with fresh produce. They will save you bones for stock, put prime fish by when they know you are coming in, and order you in something special.

'Fish is all about the moment.'

Tim Hughes, Chef Director,
J Sheekey.

Next, try to follow the seasons. Eat each fish when it is at its best: mackerel, salmon or sea trout in the summer; cod and pollack in the winter, maybe sprats when they smell sweet like cucumber. If you can, avoid flatfish such as plaice and Dover sole in the first few months of the year when producing roe eats up their energy and makes their flesh pappy. Leave them to spawn; a female cod for instance will lay more than 4 million eggs, of which only a handful will become adult fish and the rest will be food for other sea species. Again, ask the advice of your fishmonger, they will be well versed on the seasonality and availability of fish; though this book will guide you too.

The garnishes you choose, like the wine, should always complement your choice and not overshadow it. Try steamed sea kale or purple sprouting broccoli in the spring; classic samphire or asparagus and new potatoes with organic or wild salmon in the summer. Serve your sea bass with shellfish, Mediterranean-style with tomatoes or artichokes, or a firm-fleshed John Dory or brill with musky, meaty ceps in the autumn. Firmer fish can take a fiercer treatment – we serve monkfish in a fabulous fish curry and as a Milanese-inspired 'osso bucco' with gremolata. But remember the fish is always the hero of the dish.

Shellfish is often best tasting only of itself: native West Mersea or Whitstable oysters should be eaten only raw as they come from the sea, though more robust all-year-round rocks can be poached with peppery watercress soup or in Champagne to be served with scrambled egg. A plump scallop is at its sweetest when patted dry and simply steamed, roasted or grilled. We pan-fry them with creamed cauliflower, bacon and wild garlic, or cook them in the

Sea bass, line-caught off the Devon coast

shell to be served with chilli and garlic butter. Let the flavours sing and try not to smother them.

Remember, cooking fish is not complicated; the key is not to overcook it on too high a heat or for too long. You want to keep the flesh springy and succulent. Most fish is wild, from the last wilderness left in the world, and can take a lot of time, money and effort to catch.

Fish can be expensive so it needs to be treated with respect, cooked simply and quickly. Poaching or roasting a fillet of brill, say, or cod will take only minutes, and most of the recipes in this book can be prepared and cooked in a minimum amount of time.

With oily fish, it's important to season, cook it skin-side down until the delicious skin crisps, and then flip the fish over for the final few moments,

Pollack

allowing it to rest a little before serving. With white fish, cook on both sides, emphasising the skin side, so that here, too, the skin becomes crisp. With prime flat fish such as brill, plaice, lemon sole, turbot or Dover sole, we believe the best (really, the only) way to cook it is on the bone, with or without its skin. As with any meat, it is the bone that keeps the flesh deliciously moist.

The dishes in this book are from the best that Britain's most-loved fish restaurant has gathered: perfect tried-and-tested recipes that have been refined over more than 100 years of cooking the finest fish from our seas. J Sheekey takes pride in the fact our fish comes from British or close European waters and that most of our recipes are centred in the same tradition. We are happy to draw influences from other, further-away countries and their cooking and flavours, too, of course, and believe our monkfish curry, for instance, bears comparison with the best southern Asia has to offer.

The recipes for our famous fish pie, for lemon sole belle meunière from the days of Louis Saulnier's *Répertoire de Cuisine,* for lobster thermidor or for our simple deep-fried haddock, chips and mushy peas have changed little if at all since we first served them. Now, for the first time, the experience and expertise of a century of J Sheekey chefs are available to you too.

Our fish are responsibly caught from sustainable sources in British and European waters. Please ensure as best you can that yours are too.

FOOD WORTH FIGHTING FOR

SUSTAINABILITY AND J SHEEKEY

THE SUCCESS of Hugh Fearnley-Whittingstall's Fish Fight, with 800,000 signatures opposing the 'kill-it-while-you-can' style of fishing that informs much of EU fishing policy, helped bring home to many consumers what J Sheekey has practised for years: that fish we eat must be responsibly caught and from sustainable sources.

The restaurant works together with monitoring groups such as The Marine Conservation Society and Fish2Fork, a campaigning guide set up in the wake of the award-winning documentary, *The End of the Line*. Fish2Fork rates J Sheekey 4.5 'blue fish' out of 5, the highest rating Fish2Fork has so far awarded.

'We are very conscious about overfishing and discards,' says J Sheekey Chef Director, Tim Hughes. 'We are proud to be able to say where our fish is from and that it's from sustainable sources.' Concern about stocks prompted us to remove eel, skate and huss from the menu, and we ensure staff are aware of the provenance of the fish we serve, in order to be able to answer customer queries.

However, there is good news. North Sea and English Channel cod stocks are showing signs of coming back, albeit as yet at a smaller size than before; Norway has banned dredging, and recent years have seen the return of the 'artisan fisherman'. These men and women use sustainable methods – hand-gathered, creel-caught, line-fished – they are the 'organic farmers' of the sea, such as Guy Grieve of the Ethical Shellfish Company on the Isle of Mull, who supplies hand-dived king scallops and creel-caught langoustines to J Sheekey in London just 12 hours after landing them.

Grieve is passionate about the responsibilities of his role as a 'steward of the shores' and urges that fish is the most political of foods, at the centre of the debate about the way we eat, how our food is supplied and why. Grieve re-introduces thousands of small and extra-large scallops to the sea to spawn, ensuring future stocks. 'Fish is the most mysterious food we eat, from a wilderness habitat we still know little about. We must learn to cherish it.'

J Sheekey prides itself on knowing the source of its fish and so should you. Start by supporting a good fishmonger. Ask where your fish is from and if it was responsibly caught. If the answer is no, perhaps walk away and consider finding another supplier. Start to think about what fish you eat and where, the questions you should ask. Politicians are sensitive to public opinion; witness their rush to be seen to respond to Hugh's Fish Fight.

The past decade has seen a quantum shift in public attitudes to 'alternative' British fish, such as under-appreciated pollack and gurnard. J Sheekey has spent many years familiarising itself with the best of these and refining recipes for them, some of which appear in this book. Be adventurous, trust us, try them, we know what we are doing.

SHELLFISH

RAZOR CLAMS WITH CHORIZO AND BROAD BEANS

Perhaps the most striking-looking of clams, the name comes from the resemblance to a cut-throat razor. Traditionally collected when the spring tides exposed their habitat, now in Scotland they are often dived for. Order well in advance from your trusted fishmonger.

SERVES 4

RAZOR CLAMS	8, live, good-sized
FLAT LEAF PARSLEY	½ small bunch, stalks retained, leaves chopped
SHALLOTS	2, finely sliced
WHITE WINE	100ml
EXTRA VIRGIN OLIVE OIL	1 tbsp
COOKING CHORIZO	1, around 150g, cut to ½cm slices
BROAD BEANS	100g, podded
SALT AND FRESHLY GROUND BLACK PEPPER	
LEMONS	2
	FOR THE GARLIC BUTTER
UNSALTED BUTTER	150g
GARLIC	6 cloves, peeled and crushed

Firstly make the garlic butter. Mix the crushed garlic into the butter. Roll in Clingfilm and keep in the fridge until required. It will keep for up to 2 weeks and can be frozen.

Cook the broad beans in salted boiling water for 3 minutes. Drain in a colander, plunge into cold water and drain again. If they are large, pop the skins off with your fingers. If not, they'll be fine unpeeled.

Now prepare the razor clams. Start by washing them in cold running water for 10 minutes. Place the clams, parsley stalks, shallots and white wine in a saucepan. Cover with a lid and cook on a high heat for 2 minutes until all the shells have slightly opened. It is important not to overcook the clams or they will toughen. Drain in a colander.

Carefully remove the clams from their shells, keeping aside the intact shell to be used for serving. To prepare the clams, cut away the dark-looking sack and discard, slicing each into 3 or 4 pieces.

Add olive oil to a heavy-bottomed frying pan and gently fry the chorizo for a couple of minutes. Add the clams, broad beans, parsley and 20g garlic butter. Stir well, checking the seasoning. Place the shells on plates and load them with the clam and chorizo mix. Serve with halved lemons.

It's useful to have a supply of garlic butter in the fridge or freezer, which is why we've made a little more than required for this recipe. It's good for finishing dishes.

GREEN ASPARAGUS WITH SOFT-BOILED EGGS AND BROWN SHRIMPS

SERVES 4

FREE RANGE EGGS	4, medium
GREEN ASPARAGUS	500g medium, half-peeled, woody stems removed
BROWN SHRIMPS OR PRAWNS	120g, peeled and cooked
CHIVES	1 bunch, finely chopped

FOR THE DRESSING

WHITE WINE VINEGAR	1 tbsp
EXTRA VIRGIN OLIVE OIL	3 tbsp
SUNFLOWER OIL	2 tbsp
CASTER SUGAR	1 tsp
LEMON	½, juiced
SALT AND FRESHLY GROUND BLACK PEPPER	

For the dressing, place all the ingredients into a jar and shake until emulsified.

Boil 2 saucepans of water. Carefully place the eggs into one with a slotted spoon. Cook for 6 minutes. Remove to a plate. Salt the water in the other pan and add the asparagus. This will take about 5 minutes to cook. Carefully peel the eggs (you can dip them in cold water for a second or so to make this easier).

Check the asparagus is tender by cutting a little off the thick end to see if the knife cuts through it easily. Drain in a colander. Arrange on warmed plates. Cut the soft-boiled eggs in half and place on top of the asparagus.

Place the brown shrimps, chives and dressing into a saucepan and gently warm for no more than 30 seconds.

Spoon the shrimp dressing over the asparagus and serve.

POTTED SHRIMPS

This is a good simple starter that can be made the same day, or a few days before. We use Morecambe Bay shrimps, but any peeled brown shrimps work well. Order peeled shrimps from your fishmonger in advance, as it will take you the best part of a day to peel enough for a family of four. Note: here we mix everything together, rather than seal the shrimps with spiced butter.

SERVES 4

UNSALTED BUTTER	100g
LEMON	1
GROUND MACE	Pinch
CAYENNE	To taste
ANCHOVY ESSENCE	40ml
BROWN SHRIMPS	200g, peeled and cooked
SALT AND FRESHLY GROUND BLACK PEPPER	

Place the butter in a saucepan with the juice of half the lemon, ground mace, Cayenne and anchovy essence. Simmer on a low heat for 2 to 3 minutes for the spices to infuse the butter. Remove and allow the mixture to cool until just warm.

Add the shrimps to the butter mixture. Stir well and check seasoning. Pack the shrimps into ramekins or small Kilner jars and put in the fridge to set.

Remove from the fridge at least an hour before required and serve with toast and lemon wedges.

SPICED TIGER PRAWNS WITH MANGO AND CORIANDER SALSA

The mango and coriander salsa makes a fresh and spicy marriage to the tiger prawns. A light and perfect lunch or supper.

SERVES 4

TIGER PRAWNS	20, shelled and deveined
LEMON AND CHILLI SALT	To season
EXTRA VIRGIN OLIVE OIL	Splash

FOR THE CHILLI JAM

RED ONION	200g, sliced
FRESH GINGER	120g, grated
MILD CHILLI	4 medium, deseeded and chopped
PLUM TOMATOES	400g fresh, chopped
GARLIC	4 cloves, peeled and crushed
RED CHILLI FLAKES	1 tbsp
CASTER SUGAR	200g
BROWN SUGAR	40g
RICE WINE VINEGAR	250ml
FISH SAUCE	20ml
EXTRA VIRGIN OLIVE OIL	15ml

FOR THE MANGO AND CORIANDER SALSA

MANGO	1 green or under-ripe, peeled and finely diced
RED PEPPERS	2, deseeded and finely diced
MILD CHILLI	1 medium, deseeded and finely chopped
EXTRA VIRGIN OLIVE OIL	50ml
SALT AND FRESHLY GROUND BLACK PEPPER	
LEMON	½, juiced
CORIANDER	½ small bunch, finely chopped

Firstly make the chilli jam. Place all the ingredients (except the olive oil) into a heavy-bottomed saucepan. Bring to the boil and cook on a medium heat for 30 to 40 minutes until soft. Remove from the heat and liquidise until smooth. Return to the saucepan and continue to cook on a low heat for a further 10 minutes.

Place the chilli jam into a covered bowl or Kilner jar, cover with the olive oil and put into the refrigerator to cool. This can be made well in advance and be used for many different dishes.

Then make the mango and coriander salsa. Mix the mango, red pepper, chilli and olive oil in a bowl. Season, add the lemon juice and chopped coriander.

Finally, prepare the tiger prawns. Heat a splash of oil in a griddle pan or a heavy-bottomed frying pan. Sprinkle the tiger prawns with the lemon and chilli salt. Cook for 3 to 4 minutes on each side, being careful not to burn them.

To serve, place a spoonful of chilli jam on each plate and arrange the tiger prawns on top. Finish with the salsa.

LEMON AND CHILLI SALT

LEMON	1, peeled and rind retained
MILD CHILLI	8 medium, halved and deseeded
SEA SALT	4 tbsp
CASTER SUGAR	2 tbsp
	FOR THE STOCK SYRUP
WATER	100ml
CASTER SUGAR	100ml

First prepare the stock syrup by combining the water and sugar in a saucepan. Bring it to the boil, stirring occasionally, until the sugar has dissolved. This should take 5 minutes.

Pre-heat the oven to 110°C / gas mark ¼.

Add the lemon rind to the stock syrup and poach for 10 minutes. Drain the rind, discarding the stock syrup, and pat dry on kitchen roll.

On one half of a baking tray, spread out the rind, and on the other half arrange the chillis. Place in the oven until dry and crispy. This will take about 6 hours.

When both chillis and lemon rind are dry, use a grinder, hand blender or food processor to blend with the salt and sugar until it resembles a powder. Store in an air-tight container until needed.

MUSSELS WITH CIDER AND GLOUCESTER OLD SPOT BACON

Our homage to the West Country, with Devon mussels, Somerset cider and Gloucester Old Spot bacon. A British take on *moules marinières*.

SERVES 4

MUSSELS	2kg, live
EXTRA VIRGIN OLIVE OIL	30ml
ONION	1 small, peeled and finely chopped
GARLIC	1 clove, peeled and crushed
GLOUCESTER OLD SPOT STREAKY BACON	100g, chopped (however, any good quality bacon is fine)
THYME	1 sprig
DRY CIDER	150ml
DOUBLE CREAM	100ml
FLAT LEAF PARSLEY	1 small bunch, chopped
SALT AND FRESHLY GROUND BLACK PEPPER	

Prepare the mussels by washing them in cold water, scrubbing with a brush if necessary and removing the beards. If the mussels are open, pinch them. If they do not close, discard them.

In a large heavy-bottomed saucepan (you may need to cook in 2 batches as this is a generous portion), add the oil and gently cook the onion, garlic, bacon and thyme until soft. Add the mussels and cider. Cover with a lid and cook on a high heat, giving an occasional stir, until the mussels have opened. Add cream, parsley and check seasoning. Bring to the boil for a minute and serve immediately.

COCK CRABS * TOP CATCH LTD * PAIGNTON *

It is something of a mystery why south Devon crabs are the best in the world. After all, the crab has likely worked its way from Biscay, up the English Channel, past Start Bay, south of Dartmouth, as far, some say, as Dungeness in Kent or further, before its long return journey in the autumn. But ask the Chinese who buy and fly them straight off the crabbers from Dartmouth, or James Cornwall, Head Chef at J Sheekey who buys them for our fruits de mer. Or ask Kevin Bartlett who supplies the restaurant with all its live jack (cock) crabs. Dartmouth crabs are sweeter, bigger and better than the others, and have been since long before Bartlett's grandfather sold them to tourists off the sandy beach at Paignton.

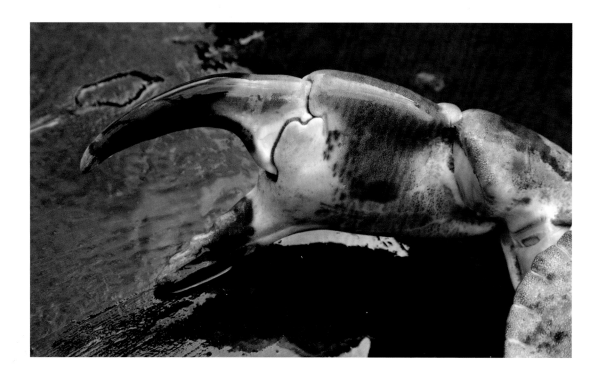

Bartlett will tell you it is because of the nutrients washing off the moor and red Devon soil into the rich rivers and out to the sea off Start Point. He will say it's because the crab grounds are protected from the chains of scallop dredgers and from being snarled in the nets of Brixham trawlers. He will tell you it is due to generations of dedicated crabmen, like Simon Mitchelmore, who lays out 1,400 pots, primed with half a tonne of gurnard (only the best bait will do), six days a week on the *Excel DH71* built by Kevin

Bartlett's grandfather. You can feel the pride both men have in their heritage, the immaculate boat and the sustainable local seafood they work hard to supply. But perhaps the real test is to visit us one day, see Bartlett's jack crabs on display, try the dishes the chefs prepare. Until then, order south Devon crab from your fishmonger, cook from our recipes here (see pages 34-44), make your own fruits de mer (see page 76). You will discover some of the sea's mysteries have to be eaten to be solved.

HOW TO PREPARE CRAB

1 Twist off legs and claws.

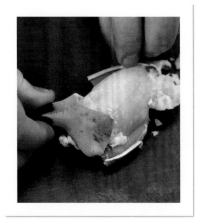

2 Crack open the claws and carefully remove the white meat, keeping it in large chunks.

3 Lift up the pointed tail on the crab's body by snapping it back with your fingers.

4 Break the shell by pressing down on each side of the body with your thumbs.

5 Lift the body section out of the shell and remove the feathery looking gills (the dead man's fingers). Discard.

6 Split the body in half with a heavy knife.

7 Now you need to be patient. Pick white meat from the leg joints and other small cavities in the body and add this to the rest of the white meat.

8 Remove the brown meat from around the inside edges of the shell.

DRESSED CRAB

The history of spicing and dressing crab meat and returning the flesh to the shell goes back deep into the Middle Ages. A perennial favourite, this recipe has been on the menu for decades.

FOR THE CRAB MAYONNAISE	
BROWN CRAB MEAT	150g
TOMATO KETCHUP	1 tsp
WORCESTERSHIRE SAUCE	1 tsp
ENGLISH MUSTARD	2 tsp
LEMON	½, juiced
WHITE OR BROWN BREAD	3 slices, crusts removed and broken into small pieces
SUNFLOWER OIL	50ml
EXTRA VIRGIN OLIVE OIL	50ml
SALT AND FRESHLY GROUND BLACK PEPPER	
WHITE CRAB MEAT	300g
FREE RANGE EGG YOLKS	2 medium, hard-boiled for 10 minutes and grated
WHOLEMEAL OR STONE BAKED BREAD	Sliced and toasted

Make the mayonnaise the day before you plan to serve it. Place the brown crab meat, egg yolks, ketchup, Worcestershire sauce and mustard into a blender and process until smooth. Add lemon juice and bread. Process again until the mixture is smooth, stopping the machine occasionally to give it a stir.

Very slowly trickle the oil into the blender, processing on a low speed as you pour. Stop the machine occasionally to scrape down the sides with a spatula and stir.

When the mayonnaise is smooth, empty it into a bowl and season if necessary. Cover with Clingfilm and refrigerate overnight.

At J Sheekey we present this in an oval mould to emulate the shape of a crab shell. The best way to serve this at home is on individual plates with equal portions of white crab meat, accompanied by the egg and brown crab mayonnaise. Serve with wholemeal toast.

CRAB BISQUE

The name bisque is thought to have come from the Biscay region. If you can't find whole crabs use raw prawns with the shells and heads on and follow the recipe in the same way.

SERVES 4–6

CRAB	1kg, live
SUNFLOWER OIL	2 tbsp
ONION	1 small, peeled and roughly chopped
LEEK	1 small, roughly chopped and washed
CARROT	1 small, peeled and roughly chopped
GARLIC	3 cloves, peeled and roughly chopped
FENNEL SEEDS	½ tsp
THYME, TARRAGON AND DILL	3 sprigs each
BAY LEAF	1
UNSALTED BUTTER	40g
TOMATO PUREE	2 tbsp
WHITE WINE	125ml
PLAIN FLOUR	3 tbsp
FISH STOCK	1.5 litre
DOUBLE CREAM	100ml
COGNAC	Splash
SALT AND FRESHLY GROUND BLACK PEPPER	

Bring a large saucepan of water to the boil. Plunge the crab into the boiling water, bring back to the boil and cook for 2 minutes. Remove the crab from the pan. Allow it to cool and then place in a heavy-duty plastic bag. Use a rolling pin to bash the body and legs into small pieces. Doing this in a plastic bag stops shell flying everywhere.

Heat the oil in a large heavy-bottomed saucepan, add the crab pieces and cook over a high heat for about 5 minutes, stirring every so often. Add the onion, leek, carrot, garlic, fennel seeds and herbs, and continue cooking for another 5 minutes or so, until the vegetables begin to colour.

Add butter and stir well. Add tomato purée, stir well and cook for a minute or so over a low heat. Increase the heat and add the wine, letting it reduce by half. Add the flour, stirring well. Slowly add the fish stock (see page 37, but a good quality cube is fine), stirring continuously to avoid lumps. Bring to the boil and season. Simmer gently for 45 minutes.

Drain the soup in a colander over a bowl, pressing down with the back of a spoon to extract all the liquid. Remove about one third of the softer white body shells (not the very hard claw and main shell) and place in with the soup. Check for any remaining meat, and keep to one side before discarding the rest. Blend shells and liquid in a liquidiser or strong food processor until smooth, then strain through a fine-meshed sieve.

Return the soup to a clean pan and re-heat. Add the cream, reserved crab meat and Cognac. Adjust the seasoning again and stir well. Serve in warm bowls with warm crusty bread and butter.

FISH STOCK

(yields approximately 2 litres of fish stock)

WHITE FISH BONES	4kg
LEEK	1, trimmed, washed and chopped
ONION	1, peeled and chopped
CELERY	1 head, chopped
FENNEL SEEDS	1 tsp
BLACK PEPPERCORNS	10
THYME	Few sprigs
BAY LEAF	1
DRY WHITE WINE	125ml
WATER	2.4 litres, cold
LEMON	1, sliced thickly
PARSLEY OR PARSLEY STALKS	Small bunch
SUNFLOWER OIL	For frying
SALT AND FRESHLY GROUND BLACK PEPPER	

You should be able to get bones from your fishmonger, particularly if asking them to fillet a whole fish.

Wash the bones in cold water. In a heavy-bottomed saucepan, heat a splash of oil and lightly cook the onion, leek, celery, fennel seeds, peppercorns, thyme and bay leaf, without allowing them to colour.

After 5 minutes, add the fish bones and wine. Bring to the boil and reduce by half. Add the water, bring to the boil again, occasionally skimming off any scum that forms. Simmer gently for 20 minutes.

Remove from the heat, add the lemon and parsley and leave to infuse for 20 minutes. Strain everything through a sieve and check seasoning. The stock will keep in the fridge for 5 days, or you can freeze it in cubes until required.

DORSET CRAB ON TOAST WITH CRUSHED BROAD BEANS, PEA SHOOTS AND LEMON DRESSING

Created for sharing plates for the opening of the J Sheekey Oyster Bar. A fresh late-spring dish for when broad beans come into season.

SERVES 4

BROAD BEANS	100g, podded
MAYONNAISE (*SEE PAGE 56*)	60ml
BROWN CRAB MEAT	50g
WHITE CRAB MEAT	200g
MILD CHILLI	1 medium, deseeded and finely chopped
PEA SHOOTS OR ROCKET	40g, washed and dried
SOURDOUGH OR COUNTRY BREAD	4 slices, toasted

FOR THE LEMON DRESSING

WHITE WINE VINEGAR	1 tbsp
EXTRA VIRGIN OLIVE OIL	3 tbsp
EXTRA VIRGIN COLD PRESSED RAPESEED OIL	2 tbsp
LEMON	½, juiced
SALT AND FRESHLY GROUND BLACK PEPPER	

For the dressing, place all the ingredients into a jar and shake until emulsified.

Cook the broad beans in salted boiling water for 3 minutes. Drain in a colander, plunge into cold water and drain again. If they are large, pop the skins off with your fingers. If not, they'll be fine unpeeled. Roughly chop them.

In a bowl, mix the mayonnaise with the brown crab meat and season.

In a separate bowl, mix together the white crab meat, chilli, chopped broad beans and toss in half of the dressing.

To serve, spread the brown crab mayonnaise liberally on the toast. Place the white crab mixture on top. Garnish with pea shoots or rocket tossed in the other half of the dressing.

BAKED SPICED CRAB WITH TOASTED SOURDOUGH

A Spanish-influenced crab dish with sherry and garlic, similar to those you might find in the tapas bars on the northern coast of Spain.

SERVES 4

EXTRA VIRGIN OLIVE OIL	100ml
ONION	1 small, peeled and finely chopped
GARLIC	1 clove, peeled and crushed
FRESH GINGER	2cm piece, peeled, finely chopped or grated
MILD CHILLIS	2 medium, deseeded and finely chopped
FINO OR MANZANILLA SHERRY	40ml
FISH STOCK	50ml
BROWN CRAB MEAT	200g
FRESH WHITE BREADCRUMBS	50g
LEMON	½, juiced
WHITE CRAB MEAT	100g
SALT AND FRESHLY GROUND BLACK PEPPER	
SOURDOUGH BREAD	Sliced and toasted, or baguette

Gently heat a heavy-bottomed saucepan with 30ml olive oil. Add the chopped onion, garlic, ginger and chilli and cook over a low heat until soft, but still pale in colour.

Increase the heat and add the sherry, allowing it to boil and reduce by half. Remove from the heat. Stir in the fish stock (see page 37, but a good quality cube is fine) and brown crab meat and mix well.

Add most of the breadcrumbs (reserving some to scatter on top), half the lemon juice and season. Return to the heat and simmer for 15 minutes, stirring occasionally.

Put one third of the mixture into a blender with the rest of the olive oil. Blend and stir back into the remaining mixture, along with the white crab meat. Add the rest of the lemon juice and season to taste.

Spoon the mixture into an oven-proof serving dish and scatter the rest of the breadcrumbs on top. Lightly brown under the grill or in a hot oven.

Serve with thin slices of toasted sourdough or a warm baguette.

FRIED COURGETTE FLOWERS WITH CRAB, TOMATO AND LEMON DRESSING

Courgette flowers can be found in the summer in good farmers' markets, specialist stores and 'pick your own' farms. Pumpkin flowers would work well too.

SERVES 4

SUNFLOWER OIL	For frying
COURGETTE FLOWERS	4
PLAIN FLOUR	20g
BEER BATTER	½ quantity (see page 152)
BASIL	½ small bunch
FRESHLY GRATED PARMESAN	20g
SALT AND FRESHLY GROUND BLACK PEPPER	

FOR THE CRAB, TOMATO AND LEMON DRESSING

EXTRA VIRGIN OLIVE OIL	6 tbsp
WHITE BALSAMIC VINEGAR	2 tbsp
LEMON	½, juiced and grated
PLUM TOMATOES	6, deseeded and diced
RED ONION	1 medium, peeled and finely chopped
WHITE CRAB MEAT	200g
SALT AND FRESHLY GROUND BLACK PEPPER	

To make the dressing, mix the oil, vinegar, lemon juice and zest together in a bowl. Add the tomatoes, red onion and white crab meat. Mix well and season. Leave to one side.

Pour 6cm of oil into a medium-sized heavy-bottomed saucepan, or use a deep fat fryer. Heat to 160°C. If using a saucepan, please be careful as the oil will be very hot. Carefully dust the flowers in flour. Dip them in batter and fry until golden brown. Remove with tongs and place onto kitchen paper to soak up excess oil. Season.

To serve, spread the crab dressing in a large serving dish, placing the courgette flowers on top. Scatter with torn basil and freshly grated Parmesan.

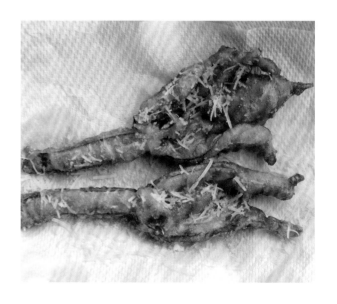

STEAMED SHELLFISH (COCKLES, MUSSELS, CLAMS, CRAB)

A dramatic dish for a family supper or small dinner party and much easier to prepare than you think. Serve it from a pan in the middle of the table with good bread to mop up the juices.

SERVES 4

COCKLES	200g, live
MUSSELS	400g, live
CLAMS	200g, live
EXTRA VIRGIN OLIVE OIL	30ml
ONION	1 small, peeled and finely chopped
GARLIC	1 clove, peeled and crushed
THYME	1 sprig
WHITE WINE	125ml
DOUBLE CREAM	100ml
WHITE CRAB MEAT	100g
BROWN CRAB MEAT	50g
FLAT LEAF PARSLEY	½ small bunch, chopped
TARRAGON	4 sprigs, leaves removed and chopped
DILL	4 sprigs, chopped
SALT AND FRESHLY GROUND BLACK PEPPER	

Prepare the shellfish by washing the cockles, mussels and clams in cold water. Scrub with a brush, if necessary, and remove the beards from the mussels. If any of the shells are open, pinch them a few times. If they do not close, discard them.

In a large heavy-bottomed saucepan (you may need to do this in 2 batches), add olive oil and gently cook the onion, garlic and thyme until soft.

Add the cockles, mussels, clams and white wine. Cover with a lid and cook on a high heat, stirring occasionally until the shells have opened. Discard any that are not open.

Add cream, crab meat and chopped herbs and stir. Bring to the boil. Season. Serve immediately from the saucepan.

'Pass me down the big mallet, Dan,' says big Bert with an evil grin. Armed now, he smashes the spider crab, splattering its life, shell and guts over the slippery deck. Dan pulls the legs off another live crab, like a boy with a butterfly, and hands it to Bert to obliterate. To skilled south-coast fishermen like Ian 'Bert' Galbraith and Daniel Green on their small boat Forget Me Not, spider crab are an ancient enemy, hoovering up the seabed, ruining their nets. It is mid-May and the two men are running twenty 400m nets strung along the Dorset shore from Sandbanks to Bournemouth pier. Today, they are out in search of prized Dover sole but they are catching lots of long-legged crab.

Any day soon, 'the weed will stop', the sea temperature will hit 11°C, and Galbraith and Green will switch from netting sole to sea bass, which Dave Haskell and Lincoln Barton of Southwest Fisheries will also ship on to J Sheekey.

The mood was different two hours before when we had joined Jeff Lander in his bid to catch crab. To Lander, a gentle, fifth-generation lobsterman, spider crab, like the cock and queen crabs and Dorset Blue lobsters he lands, are a luxury food to be handled lovingly. (In truth, crabbers tend to despise fishermen – and vice versa – each blaming the other for fouling their kit and damaging their livelihood.)

First to be landed on Lander's Star of Hannock are cuttlefish pots packed with angry leopard-like,

beautiful invertebrates hissing and shooting ink like in a scene from a sci-fi film. Next up, a roped line of 35 crab and lobster pots from the near 600 Lander and his brother run.

The 'slave' winch lifts a steady stream of pots onto the deck. Lander works quickly, quietly, re-baiting and stacking them, removing the catch. Small and still-soft-shelled crabs are thrown back for later, the rest are sorted, sized, crated, and their claws 'French cut'. Exquisite lobsters are delicately placed in upright tubes. To watch a 'Dorset blue' lifted from the waves is like looking though a sunlit stained-glass window. We stand transfixed by the iridescent turquoise, amethyst, lapis lazuli colours that saturate its shell.

HOW TO PREPARE LOBSTER

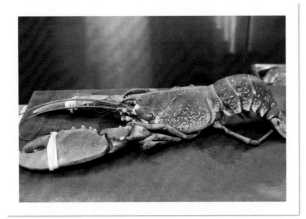

1   Carefully place the lobster into boiling court bouillon (see page 50) and cook for 10 minutes. After cooking and cooling, place the lobster right side up on a clean surface.

2   Remove the claws from the lobster.

3   Crack them open.

4   Remove the meat from the claws.

5   Remove the meat from the knuckles.

6   Insert a knife into the 'cross' in the centre of the head.

7   Cut the whole body including head and tail in half lengthways.

8   Remove the meat from the tail.

LOBSTER MAYONNAISE

Our most popular lobster dish. If you are short for time, squeamish or serving more than two, you can of course buy pre-cooked lobster and simply prepare the mayonnaise and relish.

SERVES 2

LOBSTER	1 x 500g, live
LEMON	1
MAYONNAISE (*SEE PAGE 56*)	150ml

FOR THE TOMATO AND HORSERADISH RELISH

TOMATOES	1 x 400g tin, chopped
TOMATO PUREE	40g
FRESH HORSERADISH ROOT	40g, grated
WHITE WINE VINEGAR	40ml
TOMATO KETCHUP	150g
HORSERADISH	60g, creamed
DIJON MUSTARD	1 tsp
SALT AND FRESHLY GROUND BLACK PEPPER	

FOR THE COURT BOUILLON

ONION	1 small, peeled and diced
CARROT	1, peeled and diced
LEEK	1, thinly sliced and washed
CELERY	1 stick, diced
FLAT LEAF PARSLEY STALKS	Small handful
THYME	1 sprig
BAY LEAF	1
BLACK PEPPERCORNS	5
FENNEL SEEDS	1 tsp
STAR ANISE	1
WATER	2 litres
SALT	To taste
WHITE WINE VINEGAR	50ml

Firstly prepare the relish. In a saucepan, simmer the chopped tomatoes and tomato purée for 25 to 30 minutes until reduced by half. In another saucepan, cook the fresh horseradish in vinegar until the liquid has evaporated. Keep to one side. Mix the tomato with the horseradish and leave to cool. When cool, mix in the ketchup, creamed horseradish and mustard and season.

For the court bouillon, place all the ingredients into a large saucepan. Bring to the boil and simmer for 15 minutes.

Carefully place the lobster into the boiling court bouillon and cook for 10 minutes. Remove and leave to cool.

Cut the lobster in half through the head and tail and crack the claws. Remove the tail. See page 48 for how to prepare a lobster.

To serve, place a half lobster on each plate with half a lemon and serve with the mayonnaise and tomato and horseradish relish in separate bowls.

LOBSTER SALAD WITH AVOCADO, FENNEL AND SPICED COCKTAIL DRESSING

Always a popular summer dish when native lobsters are at the height of their season. We like to add a little chilli here to spice up the Marie Rose sauce. For a profile of one of our Dorset lobster suppliers, Southwest Fisheries, see page 46.

SERVES 4

LOBSTERS	2 x 500g, cooked, meat removed from the shell (see page 48)
FENNEL	1 bulb
WATERCRESS	Handful
ROCKET	Handful
RIPE AVOCADO	1 large, sliced
CHIVES	½ bunch, chopped into 2cm lengths
DILL	4 sprigs, chopped
SALT AND FRESHLY GROUND BLACK PEPPER	

FOR THE SPICED COCKTAIL DRESSING

MARIE ROSE SAUCE (*SEE PAGE 56*)	60ml
MILD CHILLI	1 medium, deseeded and finely chopped

FOR THE LEMON DRESSING

WHITE WINE VINEGAR	1 tbsp
EXTRA VIRGIN OLIVE OIL	3 tbsp
EXTRA VIRGIN COLD PRESSED RAPESEED OIL	2 tbsp
LEMON	½, juiced
SALT AND FRESHLY GROUND BLACK PEPPER	

Firstly make the lemon dressing. Place all the ingredients into a jar and shake until emulsified.

Then make the spiced cocktail dressing by mixing the chilli into the Marie Rose sauce.

To prepare the salad, finely shave the fennel and place into a large bowl with the watercress and rocket. Add half the lemon dressing and gently mix.

Assemble the dish by spreading a spoonful of the spiced cocktail dressing on each plate. Arrange the salad on top, interweaving pieces of the lobster meat and sliced avocado, ensuring all elements of the dish are visible to the eye. Finish with chives, dill and the rest of the lemon dressing.

LOBSTER THERMIDOR

There are conflicting stories about the origin of lobster thermidor: the *Dictionnaire de l'Académie des Gastronomes* says it was created at Restaurant Maire on boulevard Saint Denis in Paris in 1894 to mark the opening of the play *Thermidor* by Victorien Sardou about the downfall of Robespierre and the end of the Terror. Others attribute it to Léopold Mourier of the Café de Paris where chef Tony Girod, his assistant and successor, is also said to have created the recipe used today. Either way, what we know for sure is that this is a favourite dish at J Sheekey.

SERVES 4

LOBSTER	4 x 500g, live
WHITE WINE	100ml
SHALLOTS	4, peeled and finely chopped
FISH STOCK	200ml
DOUBLE CREAM	300ml
ENGLISH MUSTARD	2 tsp
GRATED CHEDDAR CHEESE	40g
FRESHLY GRATED PARMESAN	20g
SALT AND FRESHLY GROUND BLACK PEPPER	
FREE RANGE EGG YOLK	1 medium

Lobsters can grow up to 6kg. We recommend native lobsters weighing between 450g to no more than 1.5kg.

Bring a large saucepan of salted water to the boil. You will probably need to cook the lobsters in two batches, according to the size of your largest saucepan. Plunge them into the boiling water and cook for 10 minutes. Remove and leave to cool.

Meanwhile, in another saucepan, reduce the white wine with the shallots until the liquid has almost evaporated. Add the fish stock (see page 37, but a good quality cube is fine) and reduce similarly. Add 200ml double cream and the mustard and reduce by half, until the sauce is thick enough to coat the back of a spoon. Add the grated cheese and whisk until the sauce is smooth. Season and leave to cool. In a bowl, whip the remaining cream until it forms soft peaks and fold into the sauce with the egg yolk.

Pre-heat the oven to 230ºC / gas mark 8.

Mix the chopped lobster meat (see how to prepare a lobster, page 48) with the sauce and return to the shell.

Bake in the oven for 10 to 15 minutes until nicely glazed, or place under a hot grill for 5 to 6 minutes. Serve with a green herb salad (see page 210).

SHELLFISH COCKTAIL

A smarter version of the classic prawn cocktail of the '70s, with the addition of Dublin Bay prawns, crab and lobster. The perfect starter for a special occasion.

SERVES 4

PRAWNS	175g, cooked and peeled
WHITE CRAB MEAT	150g
LOBSTER	1 x 500g, cooked
ICEBERG LETTUCE	½, finely shredded
SPRING ONIONS	4, finely sliced
CUCUMBER	½, diced
DUBLIN BAY PRAWNS	4, cooked and shelled, with heads intact (for garnish)

FOR THE MAYONNAISE
(yields 330ml of mayonnaise)

FREE RANGE EGG YOLKS	2 medium
WHITE WINE VINEGAR	2 tsp
ENGLISH MUSTARD	1 tsp
DIJON MUSTARD	2 tsp
SALT	½ tsp
GROUND WHITE PEPPER	
EXTRA VIRGIN OLIVE OIL	100ml
SUNFLOWER OIL	200ml
LEMON	½, juiced

FOR THE MARIE ROSE SAUCE

MAYONNAISE	140ml
TOMATO KETCHUP	60g
TABASCO	Dash, more if you like it spicy
WORCESTERSHIRE SAUCE	Dash
LEMON	Squeeze
COGNAC	Splash
DILL	½ small bunch, chopped

Firstly make the mayonnaise to use as a base for the Marie Rose sauce. Place the egg yolks, vinegar, mustards, salt and pepper into a stainless steel or glass bowl and whisk well. Mix the sunflower and olive oils together and gradually trickle into the bowl, whisking continuously. If the mayonnaise is too thick, add a few drops of water and continue whisking. When the oil is all incorporated, taste and add more seasoning if necessary, with a dash of lemon juice at the end.

To make the Marie Rose sauce, simply mix all the ingredients together. This will yield about 200ml.

Now prepare the seafood. Remove the meat from the lobster and chop into 1cm dice. Pick through the white crab meat and discard any shell.

Mix the iceberg, cucumber and spring onions together in a bowl.

For each seafood cocktail, place a spoonful of Marie Rose sauce in the bottom of the cocktail glass. Add a few peeled prawns, then the lettuce mixture to halfway up the glass. Next, add a small amount of each shellfish and a small dollop of sauce. Add more lettuce mixture. Place the rest of the shellfish on top of the lettuce. Pour a large spoonful of sauce over the top. Serve garnished with a peeled Dublin Bay prawn.

When making mayonnaise, place a damp cloth underneath the bowl to stop it slipping while you whisk.

January 31, 2012, 2pm. Scallop fisherman Guy Grieve prepares to make his third and final dive of the day, 30 metres under the icy Scottish sea outside Tobermory on the Isle of Mull. Grieve supplies around 300 medium-sized king scallops a week to J Sheekey, the shellfish arriving in London just 12 hours after being bagged on the small inflatable boat from which he disappears over the side. In the 45 minutes he will be under water, Grieve will hopefully collect about 80 to 100 scallops and will sort and size them on board, before returning any he judges too small (or too large) to the sea. A bitter easterly wind whips up the waves near the old lighthouse, a favourite hunting spot. The boatman keeps a watchful eye on the orange buoy as it unwinds its line, the only signal there is a man below.

Grieve is passionate about scallops and the island shore's fertile fringes. 'This is the last wilderness,' he says of the undersea landscapes he forages through, almost unimaginable from the relative safety of his boat. He sees scallops as an emotive foodstuff, a graphic symbol of the fight against industrial-style dredging and the destruction of heritage and habitat. He calls his company The Ethical Shellfish Company and has joined forces with other like-minded fishermen to also supply traditional creel-caught langoustine to J Sheekey.

Inspired by the quality of the produce he supplies and the care Grieve takes in catching and transporting them, we have created recipes that allow the quality and freshness of his shellfish to shine (see pages 60 and 62). We cannot guarantee the scallops you use at home will also have travelled from sea to plate the same day, or that they will be plump shellfish hand-dived from the crystal waters surrounding Mull. However, we can guarantee these recipes do justice to the extraordinary fishermen patrolling their secret underwater world to bring a pure taste of the sea to you.

ISLE OF MULL SCALLOPS IN THE HALF SHELL WITH CHILLI GARLIC BUTTER

We source scallops from Guy Grieve's Ethical Shellfish Company on the Isle of Mull in Scotland. He dives all year round from a small inflatable craft in conditions which, he says, are 'sometimes like being waterboarded by the CIA'. For a profile of Guy Grieve, see page 58.

SERVES 4

SCALLOPS	12, good-sized in the cupped shell
SALT AND FRESHLY GROUND BLACK PEPPER	
EXTRA VIRGIN OLIVE OIL	1 tbsp
FLAT LEAF PARSLEY	½ small bunch, chopped
LEMON	½, juiced
FOR THE CHILLI GARLIC BUTTER	
UNSALTED BUTTER	125g, softened
MILD RED CHILLI	1 medium, deseeded and finely chopped
GARLIC	2 cloves, peeled and crushed

Firstly prepare the chilli garlic butter. Mix the chopped chilli and crushed garlic into the butter. Roll in Clingfilm and keep in the fridge until required (it can keep for up to 2 weeks in the refrigerator or be frozen).

Heat a frying pan until smoking. Season and oil the scallops and place in the pan flesh-side down. Cook till golden brown (approximately 3 minutes); turn them over and keep in the hot pan. If your frying pan isn't large enough, use 2 pans or do them in batches and keep them warm in the oven.

Place the chilli garlic butter in a saucepan with the chopped parsley and allow the butter to melt. Season to taste and add the lemon juice.

To serve, place the scallops on a large plate and add a spoonful of the chilli garlic butter to each scallop. Serve with bread to mop up the sauce.

> When buying scallops for this dish, ask your fishmonger to leave them attached to the cupped shell. Never soak or keep scallops in water as they will become spongy and soft.

PAN-FRIED SCALLOPS WITH CREAMED CAULIFLOWER, BACON AND WILD GARLIC

Wild garlic grows freely in British woodland and on river banks from early spring through to the end of May, and is easily identifiable by its fragrant smell and lush leaves. You can also buy it in farmers' markets, good greengrocers and specialist stores.

SERVES 4

SCALLOPS	12 medium–large, removed from the shell and cleaned
EXTRA VIRGIN OLIVE OIL	1 tbsp
UNSALTED BUTTER	80g
STREAKY BACON OR PANCETTA	60g, cut into 1cm strips
WILD GARLIC LEAVES	Handful, chopped (or 2 garlic cloves, peeled and crushed)
SALT AND FRESHLY GROUND BLACK PEPPER	

FOR THE CREAMED CAULIFLOWER

CAULIFLOWER	1 small head or ½ medium
UNSALTED BUTTER	20g
VEGETABLE STOCK	To cover
SALT AND GROUND WHITE PEPPER	

Firstly prepare the creamed cauliflower. Chop the cauliflower into small pieces, place in a saucepan with butter and pour over just enough vegetable stock (see page 70, but a good quality cube is fine) to cover. Add a pinch of salt, cover with a lid and bring to the boil. Simmer for 10 minutes, checking occasionally. Remove the lid. The cauliflower should be soft. If there is any liquid left, turn up the heat until it has almost evaporated, being careful not to let it burn. Liquidise until smooth. Check seasoning and transfer to a clean saucepan. Leave to one side.

Season and oil the scallops on both sides. Heat a non-stick frying pan until almost smoking and cook the scallops on a high heat for 2 minutes on each side. Transfer to a plate. Meanwhile, melt 20g butter and gently cook the bacon (add the garlic cloves now if you are not using wild garlic) for 2 to 3 minutes without colour. Add the rest of the butter and heat until bubbling. Add the scallops and wild garlic leaves (if using). Season.

To serve, gently re-heat the creamed cauliflower and spread a couple of tablespoons in the centre of warmed plates. Arrange the scallops, bacon and garlic mixture over the top.

If using garlic instead of wild garlic, you can add colour with a few leaves of chopped flat leaf parsley.

There is a balletic poetry about the way Mike Dawson opens his West Mersea oysters, although he may not thank you for saying so. His fingers move quickly, expertly, sensitively, like Rostropovich with a cello, feeling for the moment the heel hinge will crack, the hidden muscle give, and the shell spring free. He spins the oyster round, delicately working his narrow-bladed knife underneath the meat, careful not to cut it. Quietly smiling, he flips it, proud on the cup side, and lays another oyster on a nineteenth-century carousel, part of his collection of early oyster ware.

Mike Dawson first worked with oysters as a boy before he saved enough to buy his first boat, fishing for sea bass in the summer and herring in the winter. But then he was offered a chance to buy back into the oyster business that has thrived on the Mersea coast since Roman days. (Pliny wrote admiringly of the area's oysters, if not its people or weather.)

He credits the moody Essex marshes – it's easy to imagine Magwitch looming out of the mist – with holding the secret to the sweet minerality our chefs admire. The marshes are like sponges, he says, releasing concentrated nutrients into the narrow creek where he has his oyster lanes.

6.30am Monday through Friday, Dawson's delivery arrives at J Sheekey. Signature wooden boxes of 100 oysters, cup-side down and topped with bladderwrack: 100,000 oysters a year from one supplier. We serve his West Mersea natives naked, as they come to us, with shallot vinegar, Tabasco, lemon, buttered rye bread; perhaps with wild boar sausages and cocktail chorizo for the more adventurous.

See page 66 for our simple guide to opening an oyster. Your hands may not move with Mike Dawson's dexterity, but your oysters will taste of sweet brine and the sea, just the same.

HOW TO SHUCK AN OYSTER

1 Place a tea cloth on a board. Put the oyster with the flat side facing up and cover with the top of the cloth.

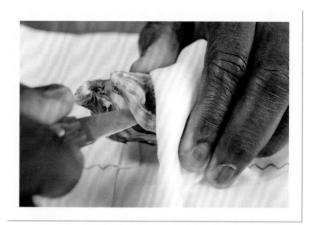

2 Using a narrow thin-bladed oyster knife, place it into the heel hinge of the oyster and move it from side to side until you hear an audible crack. This means the top shell of the oyster has been released.

3 Turn the knife so the blade is facing towards the top of the oyster shell, and at a slight angle, slide it along the top of the shell to release the top shell from the muscle. Discard the top shell.

4 Slide the oyster knife under the meat towards the muscle, being careful not to cut the flesh, and gently free the oyster from the shell.

5   It is now ready to serve.

SELECTION OF OYSTERS – natives and rocks

Wʜᴇɴ ʙᴜʏɪɴɢ ᴏʏsᴛᴇʀs, check the shells are tightly closed. They should feel full and heavy in the hand. Our oyster selection is varied and seasonal, from the British Isles and France. For a profile of our native oyster supplier, Mike Dawson of the West Mersea Oyster Company, see page 64. Speak to your fishmonger about getting hold of the varieties you prefer.

NATIVE, FLAT OR BELON OYSTERS
(ostrea edulis)

The native oyster season starts in September and runs through to April (the months with an 'r'), but we feel natives are at their best late October when they are sure to have finished spawning. We favour natives from the historic oyster beds of West Mersea, Essex and Whitstable, Kent for their characteristic mineral flavour. These deserve to be served simply naked on the shell with the accompaniment of your choice.

ROCK OR PACIFIC OYSTERS
(*crassostrea gigas*)

Available all year round, though the selection will vary. We mainly source our oysters from around the British Isles, including Jersey rocks from the Channel Isles, Lindisfarne on the Northumbrian coast, Cumbrae from the Firth of Clyde on the west coast of Scotland, Carlingford Lough from Northern Ireland, Dorset rocks from Brownsea Island and Maldon rocks from the Essex coast. We get our Fines de Claire direct from France. A bigger, bolder oyster, although perhaps lacking the intensely iodine flavour and complexity of the finest native, they respond well to poaching or other sympathetic cooking.

TO SERVE

All J Sheekey oysters are served on big platters with crushed ice and seaweed. The correct number to serve depends on fondness and appetite. Ours come with shallot vinegar (see page 76), half lemons, Tabasco and buttered rye bread. At J Sheekey, we also serve our oysters with spicy boar sausages or cocktail-sized chorizo.

VEGETABLE STOCK

We advise sticking to these vegetables, as leafy vegetables and some root vegetables will give the wrong end result.

(yields 1.5 litres)

ONIONS	3, peeled and roughly chopped
CELERY	1 small head, washed and roughly chopped
LEEK	3, trimmed, washed and roughly chopped
CARROTS	3, medium, peeled and roughly chopped
BAY LEAVES	2
THYME	2 sprigs
BLACK PEPPERCORNS	10
FLAT LEAF PARSLEY	Small bunch
FENNEL SEEDS	1 tsp
WATER	2.4 litres, cold
SALT AND FRESHLY GROUND BLACK PEPPER	

Place all the ingredients in a large saucepan and cover with water. Bring to the boil, skim off any scum that forms and simmer for 30 to 40 minutes. Strain through a sieve. Season. The stock will keep in the fridge for 5 days, or you can freeze it in cubes until needed.

WATERCRESS SOUP WITH POACHED OYSTER

Here, the pepperiness of the watercress perfectly complements the briny quality in the oyster. We would recommend high-quality rock oysters for this dish such as Fines de Claire from France or rocks from Brownsea Island, although your fishmonger will also have his own trusted suppliers.

SERVES 4

WATERCRESS	500g
UNSALTED BUTTER	50g
ONION	1, peeled and finely chopped
LEEK	1, washed and finely chopped
FLOURY POTATOES	300g, peeled and thinly sliced
VEGETABLE STOCK	1.5 litres, kept hot in a saucepan over a medium heat
SALT AND FRESHLY GROUND BLACK PEPPER	
OYSTERS	8, shucked and removed from the shell
CREME FRAICHE	100g

Remove the stalks from the watercress, retaining both stalks and leaves. In a heavy-bottomed saucepan, melt the butter and add the watercress stalks, chopped onion and leek. Cook until soft, stirring occasionally.

Add the potatoes and hot vegetable stock (see page 70, but a good quality cube is fine). Bring back to the boil, season and simmer for 10 minutes. Add the watercress leaves and cook for another 2 minutes.

Liquidise the soup until smooth and strain through a fine-meshed sieve. Re-season if necessary.

To serve, place the hot soup into bowls. Finish each with a teaspoon of crème fraîche and the shucked oyster on top.

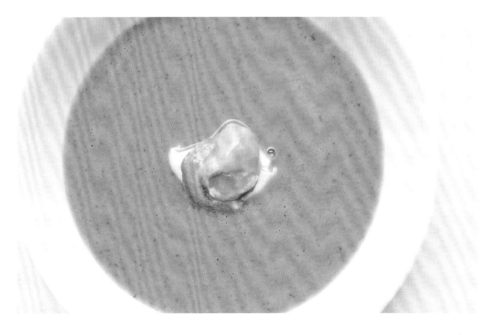

CHAMPAGNE OYSTERS WITH SCRAMBLED EGG

A dish for when you feel like spoiling yourself or others. It also works well as an appetiser. At J Sheekey, we serve this at Christmas.

SERVES 4

ROCK OYSTERS	12, shucked, juices and shells reserved
SEVRUGA CAVIAR (*OPTIONAL*)	10g

FOR THE CHAMPAGNE BUTTER SAUCE

CHAMPAGNE OR SPARKLING WINE	150ml
DOUBLE CREAM	75ml
UNSALTED BUTTER	60g, diced

FOR THE SCRAMBLED EGGS

UNSALTED BUTTER	30g
FREE RANGE EGGS	4 medium, beaten
DOUBLE CREAM	30ml
SALT AND GROUND WHITE PEPPER	

To make the sauce, bring the Champagne to the boil with the oyster juices. Simmer the oysters in the Champagne for 30 seconds and remove with a slotted spoon. Reduce the Champagne by three quarters. Add the double cream and simmer until reduced again by two thirds. Take off the heat and add the butter and stir gently until smooth. Do not let it boil. Keep in a warm place, with the oyster shells.

Next, make the scrambled eggs. Melt the butter in a heavy-bottomed pan, add the eggs and cream, and season. Stir over a low heat until the eggs are just cooked, but still on the runny side.

To serve, divide the scrambled eggs between the warmed oyster shells. Heat the oysters in the sauce, being careful not to let it boil or it will separate. Place the oyster on the scrambled egg, coat with a little sauce and finish with a teaspoon of caviar, if using.

ROASTED AND GRILLED MIXED SHELLFISH WITH GARLIC BUTTER

Shellfish porn: the ultimate feast.

(see page 32)

150g (see page 20)

SERVES 4 TO SHARE

LOBSTERS	2 x 500g, live
SUNFLOWER OIL	For frying
SALT AND FRESHLY GROUND BLACK PEPPER	
TIGER PRAWNS	8, raw
DUBLIN BAY PRAWNS	4, split in half
SCALLOPS	8, in half shell
CRAB CLAWS	4, cooked and cracked (see page 32)
GARLIC BUTTER	150g (see page 20)
SAMPHIRE	100g
FLAT LEAF PARSLEY	½ small bunch, chopped
LEMONS	2

FOR THE RAZOR CLAMS

RAZOR CLAMS	4
FLAT LEAF PARSLEY	¼ small bunch, stalks retained, leaves chopped
SHALLOT	1, finely sliced
WHITE WINE	50ml

Firstly blanch the lobsters. Bring a large saucepan of salted water to the boil (depending on the size of your saucepan, you may need to cook the lobsters in 2 batches). Plunge the lobsters into the boiling water and cook for 5 minutes. Remove from the water and leave to cool. When cool, cut each lobster in half lengthways, and crack the claws with a hammer or rolling pin. See page 48 for how to prepare a lobster.

Then cook the razor clams. Wash the clams in cold running water for 10 minutes. Place the clams, parsley stalks, shallot and white wine in a saucepan. Cover with a lid and cook on a high heat for 2 minutes until all the shells have slightly opened. Drain in a colander and leave to one side.

Heat a griddle pan until smoking. Season and lightly oil the blanched lobster. Cook for 5 minutes flesh-side down. Remove from the pan and keep warm. Wipe the pan with kitchen roll. Season and oil the tiger and Dublin Bay prawns and cook for 3 to 4 minutes on each side. Remove and keep warm. Again wipe the pan and keep hot.

Heat a heavy-bottomed frying pan until smoking. Add the oiled scallops (still inside the shell), flesh-side down. Cook for 3 minutes until golden brown. Turn over. Add the cracked crab claws and cook for 3 minutes with the scallops.

Bring a pan of unsalted water to the boil and blanch the samphire for 1 minute. Strain in a colander and keep warm.

Finally, season and lightly oil the razor clams in their shells. Place on the hot griddle pan and cook for 2 minutes. Melt the garlic butter in a saucepan and mix in the samphire and parsley.

To serve, arrange all the shellfish on a large platter and pour the garlic butter mixture over. Serve with lemon wedges.

PLATEAU DE FRUITS DE MER

You can use any shellfish that is available for this dish. The most important thing is that it is fresh and looks stunning. Below are simply some recommendations. As soon as we sell one fruits de mer the neighbouring tables start ordering it too.

SERVES 2–4

PRAWNS	200g, cooked
CRAB	1 medium, cooked, cleaned and cracked (see page 32 for how to prepare a crab)
BROWN SHRIMPS	100g, cooked
DUBLIN BAY PRAWNS	6, cooked
LOBSTER	1 x 500g, cooked
WHELKS	300g, cooked in 1 litre court bouillon (see page 50) for 30 minutes and served in their shell
CLAMS	200g, live
MUSSELS	200g, live
RAZOR CLAMS	2, live
COCKLES	200g, live
WHITE WINE	100ml

FRUITS DE MER TO BE SERVED RAW

ROCK OYSTERS	10, opened
SCALLOPS	2, raw and sliced (served in their shell)

FOR THE SHALLOT VINEGAR
(see tip)

RED WINE VINEGAR	300ml
SHALLOTS	150g, peeled and finely chopped

Firstly prepare and cook the clams, mussels, razor clams and cockles. Wash them in cold running water for 10 minutes. Scrub with a brush, if necessary, and remove the beards from the mussels. In turn, place them in a large saucepan with 25ml of white wine. Cover with a lid and cook on a high heat for 2 minutes until all the shells have slightly opened. It is important not to overcook or they will toughen. Drain in a colander and discard any that have not opened. Keep to one side.

Then make the shallot vinegar by simply mixing together the 2 ingredients.

See page 32 for how to prepare a crab and page 48 for how to prepare a lobster.

To serve: arrange the shellfish on large platters with crushed ice, seaweed if you can find it, bowls of mayonnaise and Marie Rose sauce (see page 56), tomato and horseradish relish (see page 50), and the shallot vinegar.

> For the shallot vinegar, it is important to splash out and buy the best quality red wine vinegar. It makes all the difference to the taste of the shallot vinegar. At J Sheekey, we use half red wine vinegar and half Forum's solera aged Cabernet Sauvignon vinegar, which is available online and in specialist food stores such as Brindisa.

STARTERS

GULL'S EGGS WITH CELERY SALT, MUSTARD CRESS AND MAYONNAISE

Gull's eggs are very expensive but have a silky taste that is unlike anything else. The season runs from May to June, with supply heavily controlled by the RSPB. You will need to order them in advance from a game dealer or good fishmonger.

SERVES 4

GULL'S EGGS	8–12
MUSTARD CRESS	2 punnets
MAYONNAISE (*SEE PAGE 56*)	150ml

FOR THE CELERY SALT

CELERY LEAVES	150g
SEA SALT	100g

Pre-heat the oven to 110°C / gas mark ¼.

Firstly prepare the celery salt. Spread the celery leaves out on a baking tray and dry out in the oven. This should take around 6 hours. Once completely dry, put into a food processor with the sea salt and blend to a powder-like consistency or coarser if you wish. Keep in an air-tight container and use when necessary.

To prepare the gull's eggs, gently place them into a saucepan of boiling water and cook for 7 minutes. Plunge into cold water to prevent them from cooking further. Peel carefully.

To serve, arrange the mustard cress on a plate. Sit 2 to 3 eggs per portion on top of the cress, creating a circular nest. Add a small pile of celery salt next to the cress, along with a dollop of mayonnaise.

CEVICHE OF SEA BASS WITH PLANTAIN CRISPS

Ceviche is a classic Latin American dish, dating back to the Incas, using acidic fruit, usually lime, to alter the fish proteins, having the effect of cooking the fish without heat while retaining its flavour (although technically this is 'denaturing' rather than cooking). This dish originated when we opened the J Sheekey Oyster Bar and is a perfect small dish for sharing. We also serve ceviche of scallops, salmon and monkfish – although any fish with a firm texture and good protein would work.

SERVES 4

FOR THE PLANTAIN CRISPS

PLANTAIN	1 (or 2 sweet potatoes)
SUNFLOWER OIL	For frying
SALT	
CAYENNE	

FOR THE CEVICHE

SEA BASS FILLET	600g
RED ONION	1 medium, peeled and finely chopped
MILD CHILLI	1 medium, deseeded and finely chopped
LIMES	3
SALT AND FRESHLY GROUND BLACK PEPPER	
EXTRA VIRGIN OLIVE OIL	30ml
CORIANDER	½ small bunch, roughly chopped (reserve some for garnish)

Firstly prepare the plantain crisps. Peel the plantain or sweet potatoes and shave into thin strips. Pour 6cm of oil into a medium-sized heavy-bottomed saucepan, or use a deep fat fryer. Heat to 140°C. If using a saucepan, please be careful as the oil will be very hot. Cook until golden and crisp. Drain on kitchen paper and season with salt and Cayenne.

To prepare the ceviche, skin the sea bass, remove any dark meat and cut into 1cm cubes. Place in a bowl. Add the red onion, chilli, juice of 2 limes and a pinch of salt and pepper. Allow to stand for 4 minutes. Add the olive oil, chopped coriander and check seasoning.

To serve, place the sea bass mixture into an 8cm diameter metal ring to mould. Remove the ring and finish with a sprig of coriander, wedge of lime and plantain crisps on the side.

If you want a real kick to your ceviche, you can use hotter chillis or jalapeños.

DEEP FRIED WHITEBAIT WITH CAPER MAYONNAISE

Whitebait are the tender small fry of herrings and sprats. The entire fish is eaten, including head, guts and fins. Great as a snack. We also use this recipe for sprats and sand eels.

SERVES 4

FOR THE FISH

PLAIN FLOUR	4 tbsp
SALT	1 tsp, plus more to sprinkle
CAYENNE	Good pinch
MILK	125ml
FROZEN WHITEBAIT *(FRESH IS EVEN BETTER)*	300g
SUNFLOWER OIL	For frying
LEMON	1

FOR THE CAPER MAYONNAISE

CAPERS	20g
MAYONNAISE (*SEE PAGE 56*)	60ml
FLAT LEAF PARSLEY	½ small bunch, chopped

For the caper mayonnaise, chop the capers and mix into the mayonnaise with the parsley.

Then prepare the fish. Put the flour into one bowl with the salt and Cayenne, and the milk into another. Dip the whitebait in flour, shake off any excess and place in the milk. Lift from the milk, again shaking off any excess, and drop back into the flour. Repeat this process, shaking off excess flour and place the fish on a plate or tray ready to fry.

Pour 6cm of sunflower oil into a medium-sized heavy-bottomed saucepan or deep fat fryer. Heat to 160°C. If using a saucepan, please be careful as the oil will be very hot. Fry the whitebait for 2 to 3 minutes, stirring occasionally with a slotted spoon so they don't stick together. (You may need to do this in batches.) Remove and place on kitchen paper.

Arrange lemon wedges, caper mayonnaise and extra Cayenne on the side.

FRIED COD CHITTERLINGS WITH RAVIGOTE SAUCE

Similar in texture to herring milts (soft roes), cod chitterlings are the undeveloped male roe before the eggs begin to form. They have a strong restaurant following in their short season at the end of January.

SERVES 4

COD CHITTERLINGS	240g
MILK	To cover
BAY LEAF	1
THYME	2 sprigs
PLAIN FLOUR	For dusting
FREE RANGE EGG	1 medium, beaten
FRESH WHITE BREADCRUMBS	100g
SUNFLOWER OIL	For frying
SALT AND FRESHLY GROUND BLACK PEPPER	
LEMONS	2

FOR THE RAVIGOTE SAUCE

TARRAGON VINEGAR	1 tbsp
EXTRA VIRGIN OLIVE OIL	2 tbsp
EXTRA VIRGIN COLD PRESSED RAPESEED OIL	2 tbsp
DIJON MUSTARD	2 tsp
CASTER SUGAR	Pinch
FLAT LEAF PARSLEY	½ small bunch, chopped
CHIVES	½ bunch, chopped
SHALLOTS	2, finely chopped
CORNICHONS	20g, chopped
CAPERS	20g, whole
FREE RANGE EGGS	2 medium, hard-boiled and chopped
SALT AND FRESHLY GROUND BLACK PEPPER	

For the chitterlings, place in a saucepan and cover with milk, bay leaf, thyme and a pinch of salt. Bring to the boil and simmer for 2 minutes. Remove chitterlings, drain on kitchen paper and allow to cool.

For the sauce, put vinegar, oils, mustard and caster sugar into a jar and shake until emulsified. Pour into a bowl and add the chopped herbs, shallots, cornichons, capers and eggs. Stir and season.

Pour 6cm of oil into a medium-sized heavy-bottomed saucepan, or use a deep fat fryer. Heat to 160°C. If using a saucepan, please be careful as the oil will be very hot. Cut the chitterlings into bite-sized pieces. Dip in the flour, then egg, then breadcrumbs. Fry until golden brown. Remove with tongs and place onto kitchen paper to soak up excess oil. Season.

To serve, place a spoonful of the ravigote sauce on the bottom of each plate. Top with the fried chitterlings. Serve with half a lemon.

SMOKED FISH * BROWN AND FORREST LTD * SOMERSET *

Yellowing oily walls, an acrid catch in your throat, blackened, blistered doors: there is something primal to the way we react to smoke. Your brain says run, something bad has happened here. But then the background sweet and savoury notes of exquisite fish break through.

There has been wood burning almost constantly in the smoke rooms of Brown and Forrest, in the Somerset levels far from the sea, for more than thirty years. Behind the charred doors – like something from a Fire Brigade warning sign – are small spaces so intensely dark it takes your eyes time to adjust to the coral sides of fish ethereally floating on racks. No shocking pink salmon here; the fish we prize is a subdued saffron orange, the colour of Tibetan lama robes at sunrise.

The colour is a clue to the care Jesse Pattisson takes: the depth of cure, the oak smoke, the time the fish has settled in each stage before being readied to eat. Each fillet is from a 3–4kg, three-year-old fish with a developed dorsal fin that has swum in the tidal waters of Loch Duart. Sides are pre-pin-boned, a few narrow cuts carved in their skin before being dry-cured with brown sugar and salt. They are left to steep for five hours, rinsed and racked for a further fifteen to 'relax'. After smoking, they will rest overnight before being wrapped in paper (no vacuum-packing for J Sheekey, thank you), boxed and dispatched to us in London.

Our Chef Director Tim Hughes chooses a side to carve. Taking a serrated, flexible blade – the same you would use for gammon – he starts at the tail, cutting away from the head. The flesh is moist, almost aromatic, with a firm, dry texture and 'bite'. You should be able to see the blade through the flesh as you work, he says, but the length of slice is a matter of taste and tradition. As, of course, is whether you eat it served simply with bread and lemon, or as many of J Sheekey's 'old gentlemen' prefer – dressed with capers and 'red' (Cayenne) pepper.

Our recipe for smoked salmon and Parmesan straws appears in the Savouries section, on page 248, eggs Arlington on page 247.

CHILLED BEETROOT SOUP WITH HOT SMOKED SALMON AND HORSERADISH

We source all our smoked salmon from Brown and Forrest in Somerset, but hot smoked salmon is widely available from good fishmongers and can be found, usually vacuum-packed, in most supermarkets. For a profile of Brown and Forrest, see page 88.

SERVES 4

RAW BEETROOT	400g
EXTRA VIRGIN OLIVE OIL	1 tbsp
ONION	1 small, peeled and roughly chopped
LEEK	1 small, roughly chopped and washed
VEGETABLE STOCK	1 litre
BALSAMIC VINEGAR	1 tbsp
SALT AND FRESHLY GROUND BLACK PEPPER	
CREME FRAICHE	2 tbsp
CREAMED HORSERADISH	2 tbsp
HOT SMOKED SALMON FILLETS	200g, broken into bite-sized pieces

Place the beetroot (do not use pre-cooked), still in their skins, into a heavy-bottomed saucepan and cover with water. Bring to the boil and cook for 45 minutes to an hour, until tender, ensuring you keep topping up the pan with water. Drain, peel and roughly chop. Keep to one side.

Add oil to a heavy-bottomed saucepan and gently cook the onion and leek. Add the vegetable stock (see page 70, but a good quality cube is fine), bring to the boil, season and simmer for 10 minutes. Add beetroot, bring back to the boil and cook for a further 5 minutes. Remove from the heat. Liquidise until smooth, and strain through a sieve. Add more stock if needed. Leave to cool. Refrigerate for a few hours until well chilled or place into the freezer if you're in a rush.

Once the soup has chilled, stir in balsamic vinegar and re-season if necessary as the flavour changes a little when cold. In another bowl, mix together the crème fraîche and horseradish. Season to taste.

To serve, pour the soup into chilled bowls, add the hot smoked salmon and top with a spoonful of horseradish cream.

CORNISH FISH SOUP WITH SAFFRON MAYONNAISE

Our British take on the traditional French-style fish soup, typical of the medieval town of Guérande in the Pays de la Loire. Saffron has been an important ingredient in Cornish dishes for centuries and gives this soup its essential smoky, spicy element. Saffron mayonnaise also works well with grilled and barbecued shellfish and squid.

SERVES 4

FOR THE SOUP

EXTRA VIRGIN OLIVE OIL	2 tbsp
WHOLE RED MULLET	250g, gutted and roughly chopped
WHOLE GURNARD	250g, gutted and roughly chopped
WHOLE WHITING	250g, gutted and roughly chopped
FISH BONES (*YOUR FISHMONGER SHOULD GIVE YOU THESE*)	250g
ONION	1 medium, peeled and roughly chopped
LEEK	1, roughly chopped and washed
FENNEL	1 small bulb, roughly chopped
RED PEPPER	1, deseeded and roughly chopped
POTATO	1 medium, peeled and roughly chopped
GARLIC	3 cloves, peeled and chopped
SAFFRON STRANDS	Pinch
BAY LEAF	1
THYME	Few sprigs
BLACK PEPPERCORNS	1 tsp
JUNIPER BERRIES	3
TOMATO PUREE	1 tbsp
CHOPPED TOMATOES	1 x 230g tin
WHITE WINE	125ml
FISH STOCK	2 litres
SALT AND FRESHLY GROUND BLACK PEPPER	

To make the soup, heat the olive oil in a large heavy-bottomed saucepan, and gently fry the fish, bones, vegetables, spices and herbs for about 10 minutes.

Add the tomato purée. Cook for 2 minutes. Add the wine, reduce by half. Then add the chopped tomatoes and fish stock (see page 37, but a good quality cube is fine). Bring to the boil, season and simmer for 40 minutes.

Liquidise one third of the soup (bones and all), return to the saucepan and simmer gently for another 20 minutes. Strain the soup through a sieve or conical strainer. Re-season if necessary. Keep to one side.

For the saffron mayonnaise, pour 100ml of the fish soup into a saucepan, add saffron and garlic, bring to the boil and simmer for a few minutes. Add the bread and stir well. Remove from the heat and cool a little.

Pour into a blender and mix well with the egg yolk. Mix the oils together, and slowly trickle into the mixture, stopping the machine occasionally and scraping down the sides. When thick, season with salt and Cayenne and add lemon juice. Give the mixture a final blend. Transfer to a bowl.

To serve, re-heat the fish soup. Pour into warm soup bowls, and serve with saffron mayonnaise on the side and crusty bread. We serve this with grated Gruyère sprinkled over the top.

FOR THE SAFFRON MAYONNAISE

FISH SOUP	100ml
SAFFRON STRANDS	Pinch
GARLIC	2 cloves, peeled and crushed
WHITE BREAD	1 slice, crusts removed and broken into pieces
FREE RANGE EGG YOLK	1 medium
EXTRA VIRGIN OLIVE OIL	40ml
SUNFLOWER OIL	40ml
LEMON	Squeeze
SALT	
CAYENNE	

SMOKED HADDOCK AND FENNEL SOUP WITH POACHED EGG

From kedgeree to omelette Arnold Bennett, smoked haddock and egg
is a model combination. This is a comforting, perfect supper dish.
We use Burford Brown eggs for the richly coloured yolks and flavour.

SERVES 4

UNSALTED BUTTER	40g
FENNEL	1 bulb, roughly chopped
LEEK	1, roughly chopped and washed
FENNEL SEEDS	½ tsp
PLAIN FLOUR	1 tbsp
VEGETABLE STOCK	500ml
UNDYED SMOKED HADDOCK	150g, skinned
MILK	225ml
SALT AND GROUND WHITE PEPPER	
FREE RANGE EGGS	4 medium
DOUBLE CREAM	60ml
DILL	½ bunch, chopped

Heat the butter in a heavy-bottomed saucepan.
Add the fennel, leek and fennel seeds and cook
until soft. Add the flour and stir well. Gradually add
the vegetable stock (see page 70, but a good quality
cube is fine), stirring well. Bring to the boil and
simmer for 20 minutes.

Meanwhile, poach the haddock in milk for 3 to
4 minutes. Add half the fish and all the milk to the
soup and liquidise until smooth. Strain through
a sieve. Season if necessary. Keep on a low heat.

Poach the eggs. While these are cooking, gently
break the remainder of the haddock into flakes
and place into the soup with the cream and half
the chopped dill. Bring the soup to the boil for a
minute. Serve in soup bowls with the poached eggs
in the middle and finish with the rest of the dill.

> To poach eggs, bring to the boil a saucepan
> of water and add a little white wine vinegar.
> Do not add salt, as this will make the whites
> separate. Crack the eggs into a cup and gently
> pour into the water. Poach for 3 minutes.

PEA, LETTUCE AND LOVAGE SOUP AND CHEDDAR SCONES

A summery refreshing lunch or supper dish for when peas and lettuce are plentiful. Lovage, sometimes referred to as Love Parsley, is easy to grow in pots or the garden and adds depth to the classic French soup. In the past we served this with snail tortellini.

SERVES 4

FOR THE SOUP

SUNFLOWER OIL	For frying
UNSALTED BUTTER	20g
PEAS	400g, shelled or frozen
LEEK	1, cut into small pieces and washed
CELERY	2 sticks, cut into small pieces
ONION	1, peeled and finely sliced
VEGETABLE STOCK	1 litre, kept simmering in a saucepan
SALT AND FRESHLY GROUND BLACK PEPPER	
LITTLE GEM LETTUCE	2 heads, roughly chopped
LOVAGE LEAVES	5
DOUBLE CREAM	50ml

FOR THE CHEDDAR SCONES
(makes at least 8)

PLAIN FLOUR	250g
BAKING POWDER	2 tsp
SALT	1 tsp
CASTER SUGAR	1 tsp
UNSALTED BUTTER	60g, chilled and diced
MATURE CHEDDAR CHEESE	100g, grated
FREE RANGE EGG	1 medium, beaten
MILK	100ml
FREE RANGE EGG YOLK	1 medium

For the scones, pre-heat oven to 190°C / gas mark 5. Sieve the flour and baking powder together, add the salt and sugar and rub in the butter to form a fine crumb. Gently stir in most of the grated Cheddar (reserving a little for the garnish), beaten egg and milk and bring together into a dough. Allow to rest for 10 minutes.

Roll the dough to 3cm thickness and cut with a 4cm circular cutter. Place the scones onto a greased baking tray and rest again for 10 minutes.

Brush the scones with egg yolk and top with the remaining grated cheese. Bake for 8 minutes and keep warm.

To make the soup, heat the oil and butter in a heavy-bottomed saucepan and gently cook the peas, leek, celery and onion until soft. Add the boiling vegetable stock (see page 70, but a good quality cube is fine), bring back to the boil, season and simmer for 10 minutes. Remove from the heat.

Add the lettuce and lovage to the soup and liquidise until smooth. Strain and season if necessary.

To serve, re-heat the soup and stir in the double cream. Ladle into bowls and serve with warm Cheddar scones.

> When making green vegetable soups, it is best to add boiling stock to ensure the colour is retained.

ARBROATH SMOKIES AND ENDIVE SALAD WITH QUAIL'S EGGS

Arbroath Smokies are available at all good fishmongers. Alternatively, you can use any type of smoked fish: salmon, trout, mackerel or anchovy.

SERVES 4

QUAIL'S EGGS	8
ARBROATH SMOKIES	2, whole
WHITE ENDIVE	2 heads
RED ENDIVE	1 head
SHALLOTS	2, finely chopped
CHIVES	1 bunch, chopped

FOR THE GRAIN MUSTARD DRESSING

WHITE WINE VINEGAR	1 tbsp
CLEAR HONEY	1 tbsp
EXTRA VIRGIN OLIVE OIL	200ml
SUNFLOWER OIL	100ml
SWEDISH OR DIJON MUSTARD	2 tbsp
GRAIN MUSTARD	2 tbsp
SALT AND FRESHLY GROUND BLACK PEPPER	

First boil the quail's eggs for 3 minutes. Leave to cool, peel and cut in half.

For the salad, peel the Arbroath Smokies away from the bone, removing all the bones. Break into bite-sized pieces.

For the dressing, blend the first 5 ingredients together then whisk in the grain mustard at the end and season to taste.

Cut the bottoms off the endives and gently separate the leaves, putting them into a bowl. Add the shallots and lightly dress.

To serve, arrange the endive leaves in layers on a serving plate with Arbroath Smokies and quail's eggs placed in between the leaves.

Finish with more dressing and chopped chives.

PICKLED ARCTIC HERRINGS, POTATO SALAD AND DILL SAUCE

Pickled herrings are popular throughout Europe, particularly in the Baltic and Nordic regions, and can be found as far afield as Japan. We prefer this style of pickling to sousing herrings. Note that in summer, herrings may not be fatty enough to use.

SERVES 4

HERRING FILLETS	12, fresh
SALT	2 tbsp

FOR THE PICKLING LIQUID

DISTILLED VINEGAR	100ml
WATER	800ml
CASTER SUGAR	170g
PIMENTO SEEDS	3
BLACK PEPPERCORNS	6
BAY LEAVES	2
CARROTS	2 medium, thinly sliced in rounds
SHALLOTS	2, thinly sliced in rounds

FOR THE POTATO SALAD

WAXY POTATOES	1kg, peeled
MAYONNAISE (*SEE PAGE 56*)	60ml
CREME FRAICHE	1 tbsp
CHIVES	1 bunch, chopped
SALT AND FRESHLY GROUND BLACK PEPPER	

FOR THE DILL SAUCE

MAYONNAISE (*SEE PAGE 56*)	100ml
SWEDISH MUSTARD	2 tsp
DILL	Small bunch, chopped
PICKLING LIQUID	Splash

Salt the herring fillets, Clingfilm and chill overnight in the fridge. Next day, ensure they are well soaked in water to remove all the salt. This will take about an hour and you should change the water regularly. Drain and proceed with pickling.

Thoroughly mix together all the pickling ingredients. Place the herring fillets in a large, shallow dish and pour over the pickling liquid, making sure they are well covered. Cover the dish with Clingfilm and place in the fridge. The herrings will take at least 3 days before they're ready. Once ready they can last up to 2 weeks.

Remove the herrings from the pickling liquid which you should set aside for later. Roll up the fillets and secure them with cocktail sticks. Put the herrings back into the pickling liquid until needed.

Now make the potato salad. Boil the potatoes in salted water until soft. Drain and leave to cool in a bowl for 5 minutes. Roughly crush the potatoes. Mix in the mayonnaise, crème fraîche and chopped chives. Season.

Finally prepare the dill sauce. Mix all the ingredients together and adjust the consistency with some of the pickling liquid.

To serve, remove the carrots and shallots from the pickling liquid. Arrange the herrings on each plate – 1 standing up and 1 on its side – cover 1 with the dill sauce and the other with carrots and shallots. Add a tablespoon of potato salad to the plate and serve with rye or crusty bread and extra dill sauce on the side.

SMOKED ANCHOVIES, GREEN BEANS AND SOFT-BOILED EGGS

We buy our anchovies from specialist Spanish importers, Brindisa, who source them from the port of Getaria in northern Spain, where they are smoked over beechwood before being packed by hand in olive oil.

SERVES 4

FREE RANGE EGGS	4 medium
EXTRA FINE GREEN BEANS	300g, topped and tailed
SHALLOTS	2, finely sliced
RADISHES	1 bunch, shaved
WATERCRESS (OR ROCKET LEAVES)	50g
SMOKED ANCHOVY FILLETS	2 x 100g tins, drained
CHIVES	½ bunch, chopped
SALT	Pinch

FOR THE DRESSING

WHITE WINE VINEGAR	1 tbsp
EXTRA VIRGIN OLIVE OIL	3 tbsp
EXTRA VIRGIN COLD PRESSED RAPESEED OIL	2 tbsp
LEMON	½, juiced
SALT AND FRESHLY GROUND BLACK PEPPER	

For the dressing, place all the ingredients into a jar and shake until emulsified.

Put 2 saucepans of water on to boil. In one of the saucepans boil the eggs for 6 minutes. Plunge immediately into cold water and peel while warm. In the other saucepan, add salt and cook the beans for 5 minutes. Drain and plunge the beans into cold water and drain again. When cool, split the beans in half lengthways.

In a large shallow serving bowl, place the cooked green beans, shallots, radishes and watercress. Dress and toss the salad. Add the anchovies, soft-boiled eggs, cut in half, and sprinkle over the chives.

GRAVADLAX WITH MARINATED CUCUMBER AND DILL MUSTARD DRESSING

This Scandinavian speciality was historically wrapped in bark and buried as a means for salmon fishermen to preserve their catch. If you cannot find Swedish mustard – it's sweeter and without the kick most other mustards have – use French's American mustard or stick to Dijon. We sometimes use a beetroot cure, adding grated raw beetroot in with the salt.

SERVES 6–8

SIDE OF SALMON	1kg, skin on, trimmed and pin-boned
BROWN SUGAR	85g
FINE SEA SALT	65g
GROUND WHITE PEPPER	½ tsp
LIME	1, zested
SWEDISH MUSTARD	75g
DILL	Bunch, chopped

FOR THE DILL MUSTARD DRESSING

DIJON MUSTARD	1 tsp
SWEDISH MUSTARD (OR USE DIJON AND TREBLE THE SUGAR)	2 tbsp
BROWN SUGAR	2 tsp
SUNFLOWER OIL	6 tbsp
DILL	4 sprigs, finely chopped
SALT AND FRESHLY GROUND BLACK PEPPER	

To prepare the fish, lay the salmon fillet on a piece of Clingfilm large enough to wrap back over the fish. Mix sugar, salt, pepper and lime zest together in a bowl, cover the fish with the mixture and leave uncovered at room temperature for 45 minutes. Then, wrap and seal the fish in the Clingfilm, place on a tray and leave in the refrigerator for 2 days.

After two days, unwrap the salmon and discard any juices. Lightly wash it in cold water and dab dry with kitchen roll. Put it onto a fresh piece of Clingfilm. Sprinkle half the dill onto the salmon, spread with mustard, and finally the rest of the dill. Again wrap tightly and refrigerate. Best to leave for at least a day before using. It should last for up to a week.

For the dill mustard dressing, firstly whisk together the two mustards and sugar. Slowly add the oil, adjusting with a little warm water if the mixture becomes too thick. Add the dill and season to taste.

FOR THE MARINATED CUCUMBER

CUCUMBER	1, halved lengthways and deseeded
WHITE WINE VINEGAR	2 tbsp
SHALLOTS	2 large, peeled and thinly sliced
MUSTARD SEEDS	1 tsp
CASTER SUGAR	4 tsp
SALT AND FRESHLY GROUND BLACK PEPPER	
DILL	4 sprigs, finely chopped
EXTRA VIRGIN OLIVE OIL	3 tbsp

To marinate the cucumber, firstly slice it thinly at an angle and place into a bowl. Meanwhile, in a heavy-bottomed saucepan, bring the vinegar, shallots, mustard seeds, sugar, salt and pepper to the boil. Remove from the heat and leave to cool a little. Pour over the cucumber and leave at room temperature for an hour, stirring occasionally. When ready to serve, drain off the liquid and mix the olive oil and dill into the drained cucumber. Season.

Finally, to assemble the dish, unwrap the salmon and, with a long, sharp carving knife, cut slices about ½cm thick at an angle, turning the knife when you get to the skin. Place 4 slices per person (more if you like) onto a plate, adding a spoonful of the dill mustard dressing and marinated cucumber on the side.

MANX KIPPER PÂTÉ

You can use Craster, Scottish or other kippers for this dish, but we prefer the smaller, sweeter fish from the Isle of Man.

SERVES 4

MANX KIPPERS	400g
UNSALTED BUTTER	150g
CREAM CHEESE	125g
TABASCO	2 dashes
LEMON	½, juiced
TOAST	
SALT AND FRESHLY GROUND BLACK PEPPER	
CAYENNE	

Place the kippers (fillets if you prefer) into a heat-proof deep bowl with two thirds of the butter and Clingfilm over the top. Place over a boiling water bath (bain-marie) and simmer for 10 minutes. Drain the fish in a colander, keeping the juices, and allow to cool.

Once cool, separate the fish from the skin and remove as many bones as possible. Sieve the buttery juices into a bowl and add the cream cheese, Tabasco and lemon juice. Add the kipper flesh and fold it in gently, as you don't want the mixture to become a purée. Season.

Press the pâté into ramekins or rounded moulds. Lastly, melt the remaining butter (do not allow it to brown) and pour over each ramekin to seal the surface of the pâté. Serve with toast and Cayenne on the side.

GRILLED SARDINES WITH MOROCCAN SPICED SALAD

Typical of the salad served on the quayside in Essaouira on Morocco's Atlantic coast, this dish works well with other oily fish such as mackerel and anchovies. Preserved lemons are available in larger supermarkets. Ras el hanout is slightly different wherever you buy it, but tends to feature ginger, galangal, anise, cinnamon, nutmeg, cloves, cardamom, mace and turmeric, together with aromatic flowers such as lavender and rose. Good delis and most supermarkets sell it.

SERVES 4

GREEN PEPPERS	3
TOMATOES	8 medium, skinned, deseeded and diced into 1cm pieces
SPRING ONIONS	½ bunch, chopped
EXTRA VIRGIN OLIVE OIL	6 tbsp, plus more for brushing
WHITE WINE VINEGAR	2 tbsp
GARLIC	1 clove, peeled and crushed
PRESERVED LEMON	1, diced
SALT AND FRESHLY GROUND BLACK PEPPER	
SARDINES	8, gutted and cleaned
RAS EL HANOUT	2 tsp

Pre-heat the grill. Cut the peppers in 4 lengthways, remove the stalk and seeds, and place on a grill tray. Grill skin-side up for about 10 minutes or until the skin is blistering and blackening. Remove from the tray, put into a bowl, cover with Clingfilm and leave for about 10 minutes. Remove the skin with your fingers or by scraping with a knife.

Cut the skinned peppers into 1cm dice and place in a bowl with the tomatoes, spring onions, olive oil, vinegar, garlic and preserved lemon. Season and mix well. Add a little of the juice from the preserved lemon to taste.

Pre-heat the grill to its hottest temperature. Make a couple of diagonal slashes across each side of the fish, brush them with olive oil and rub ½ teaspoon of ras el hanout into each fish. Season. Grill the fish for about 3 minutes on each side until the skin begins to crisp.

Place the salad onto a large serving dish and top with the grilled sardines.

RED GURNARD SALAD WITH SAMPHIRE AND JERSEY ROYALS

British gurnard is recommended by the Marine Conservation Society in its *Good Fish Guide* (www.goodfishguide.co.uk). It also makes for superior fish fingers.

SERVES 4

EXTRA VIRGIN OLIVE OIL	2 tbsp
GURNARD FILLETS	4 x 100g, pin-boned
SAMPHIRE	100g, woody stalks removed
JERSEY ROYAL POTATOES	500g, skins scrubbed, cooked
LAND CRESS AND BABY RUBY CHARD LEAVES (*ALTERNATIVELY, USE A BAG OF MIXED BABY LEAVES*)	Large handful of each
SALT AND GROUND WHITE PEPPER	
CHIVES	½ bunch, chopped

FOR THE DRESSING

TARRAGON VINEGAR	1 tbsp
EXTRA VIRGIN OLIVE OIL	2 tbsp
EXTRA VIRGIN COLD PRESSED RAPESEED OIL	2 tbsp
DIJON MUSTARD	2 tsp
CASTER SUGAR	Pinch
GARLIC	1 clove, peeled (optional)
SALT AND FRESHLY GROUND BLACK PEPPER	

For the dressing, place all the ingredients into a jar and shake until emulsified. The whole garlic clove is used for infusion and should be removed just before use.

Next, heat olive oil in a non-stick frying pan. Season and cook the fillets, skin-side down first, for 2 to 3 minutes on each side. Remove from the pan and leave to cool. Meanwhile bring a saucepan of unsalted water to the boil and blanch the samphire for 1 minute. Strain in a colander. Slice the cooked, warm Jersey Royals into rough 1cm slices and mix in a bowl with the samphire, salad leaves and half of the dressing. Season.

Arrange the salad on plates. Break up each fish fillet into 3 or 4 pieces and place on top. Drizzle extra dressing on top and, finally, sprinkle over the chives.

MIXED BEETROOT SALAD WITH SMOKED MACKEREL AND HORSERADISH DRESSING

Here the mackerel adds a smoky layer to the classic pairing of beetroot and horseradish.

SERVES 4

RAW MIXED HERITAGE BEETROOT	400g golden, chioggia and classic red
MIXED SALAD	100g, ruby leaves ideal
RED CHICORY	1 head
SMOKED MACKEREL FILLETS	320g
FRESH HORSERADISH ROOT	2cm, grated

FOR THE DRESSING

WHITE WINE VINEGAR	1 tbsp
EXTRA VIRGIN OLIVE OIL	2 tbsp
EXTRA VIRGIN COLD PRESSED RAPESEED OIL	2 tbsp
CREAMED HORSERADISH	1 tbsp
DIJON MUSTARD	2 tsp
CASTER SUGAR	Pinch
GARLIC	1 clove, peeled (optional)
SALT AND FRESHLY GROUND BLACK PEPPER	

For the dressing, place all the ingredients into a jar and shake until emulsified. The whole garlic clove is used for infusion and should be removed just before use.

In a saucepan of boiling water, cook the beetroots in their skins (this should take about 30 to 40 minutes, depending on size) and peel while warm. Once they have cooled down, roughly chop the beetroots.

To serve, toss the beetroot pieces in half the dressing and place them on a large plate. Scatter the salad leaves and chicory between the beetroot pieces. Break the mackerel fillets into pieces and arrange over the salad. Finish with extra dressing and grated horseradish.

CORNISH MACKEREL FILLET WITH PICKLED VEGETABLES

Versatile, sustainable, spanking fresh mackerel, rich in omega oils, is supplied to us by Matthew Stevens in St Ives. Revered on the coast and continent, it has largely fallen out of favour here unless it is smoked and vacuum-packed on supermarket shelves. It is loved by chefs, who balance the fish's oiliness with acidity, such as in a sharp rhubarb sauce or pickled vegetables. This recipe will work with red and grey mullet, sea bream and sea bass. For a profile of Matthew Stevens & Son, see page 194.

EXTRA VIRGIN OLIVE OIL	SERVES 4
SALT AND FRESHLY GROUND BLACK PEPPER	For frying
MACKEREL FILLETS	4 x 100g, fresh

	FOR THE PICKLED VEGETABLES
EXTRA VIRGIN OLIVE OIL	100ml
SHALLOTS	3, thinly sliced
CARROTS	2 medium, thinly sliced
SAFFRON STRANDS	Pinch
CORIANDER SEEDS	1 tsp, crushed
GARLIC	1 clove, thinly sliced
ORANGE	1, juiced
WHITE WINE VINEGAR	50ml
WHITE WINE	50ml
CORIANDER	½ small bunch, chopped
SALT AND FRESHLY GROUND BLACK PEPPER	

Firstly prepare the pickled vegetables. Heat a generous splash of olive oil in a heavy-bottomed saucepan. Add shallots, carrots, saffron, coriander seeds and garlic. Slowly cook without colour for 5 minutes.

Add orange juice and reduce until the liquid has evaporated. Do the same with the white wine vinegar and again with the white wine. Add the rest of the olive oil and simmer for 10 minutes (do not boil). Remove from the heat and leave to cool. Season and add the fresh coriander. This part of the dish should be prepared in advance to enhance its flavour.

Prepare the mackerel. Heat the oil in a non-stick frying pan. Season the fillets and cook skin-side down. This should take around 3 minutes. Turn the fish over and take off the heat, keeping in the pan (the heat of the pan will gently cook the other side).

Warm through the pickled vegetables in a saucepan, being careful not to boil. Place the fish onto a large serving dish and cover with pickled vegetables. Serve with grilled country bread and tapenade (see page 246).

ENGLISH ASPARAGUS HOLLANDAISE

The taste of British summer, traditionally served from the beginning of May for about six weeks, though early crops from Cornwall and planting further north has extended the season past the traditional cut-off of Midsummer's Day. Cultivating asparagus can be traced to Ancient Greece, while Pliny the Elder writes admiringly of giant spears from Ravenna in the Italian region of Emilia-Romagna. For this dish we recommend medium-sized local asparagus served with a rich buttery hollandaise.

SERVES 4

GREEN ASPARAGUS	500g medium, half-peeled, woody stems removed
	FOR THE HOLLANDAISE SAUCE
WHITE WINE VINEGAR	40ml
WATER	40ml
SHALLOT	1 small, chopped
TARRAGON	2 sprigs
BAY LEAF	1
PEPPERCORNS	5
UNSALTED BUTTER	200g
FREE RANGE EGG YOLKS	3 medium
SALT AND GROUND WHITE PEPPER	

For the hollandaise, place vinegar, water, shallot, herbs and peppercorns in a saucepan and bring to the boil. Reduce the liquid by two thirds. Sieve the liquid, leave to cool and set aside.

In a heavy-bottomed saucepan, melt the butter on a very low heat until it clarifies. Skim off any white liquid that forms on the surface. Strain and keep the butter at room temperature. Put the egg yolks into a small bowl with half the vinegar reduction and whisk over a pan of gently simmering water until the mixture begins to thicken and doubles in size. Gradually pour in the butter, whisking the mixture continuously (you can use an electric hand whisk). If the butter is added too quickly, the sauce will separate. When you have added two thirds of the butter, taste the sauce and add a little more of the remaining vinegar reduction to taste (the vinegar should just cut the oiliness of the butter). Add the rest of the butter as before. Season, cover with Clingfilm and leave at room temperature until needed.

Cook the asparagus in boiling salted water for about 5 minutes or until tender. Drain and arrange on plates and serve with the hollandaise.

ASPARAGUS AND WINDRUSH GOAT'S CHEESE TART

Windrush is a British goat's cheese produced in Oxfordshire, with a slightly citrus flavour, but any soft, fresh goat's cheese should work well in this dish.

SERVES 4

GREEN ASPARAGUS	500g medium, half-peeled, woody stems removed
UNSALTED BUTTER	20g
DOUBLE CREAM	50ml
FRESHLY GRATED PARMESAN	30g
PUFF PASTRY	250g
FREE RANGE EGG	1 medium, beaten
WINDRUSH GOAT'S CHEESE	120g
PLAIN FLOUR	For dusting
SALT AND FRESHLY GROUND BLACK PEPPER	

Use any leftover pastry to make smoked salmon and Parmesan straws (see page 248).

Cook the asparagus in boiling salted water for about 5 minutes or until tender. Drain in a colander and plunge into cold water. Drain again and place to one side.

Cut the tips off the asparagus stalks (about 6cm) and leave to one side. Chop the stalks, place them into a pan with the butter and cover with cream. Bring to the boil, add the Parmesan and cook for 5 minutes. Take off the heat and liquidise.

Pre-heat the oven to 180°C / gas mark 4.

On a floured surface, roll out the pastry to around 5mm thick. Leave to rest for 15 minutes. Cut out 4 rectangles 14cm long x 9cm wide. Place on a greased baking tray, and prick all over with a fork to prevent the pastry rising too much. From the rest of the pastry, cut 1cm wide strips as long as you can. Brush the edges of the rectangles with beaten egg. Lay the strips along the 4 sides. Finally, brush the edges with egg again. Leave to rest in the fridge for 1 hour.

Bake the pastry for 7 minutes. Remove from the oven and set aside. Increase the heat to 200°C / gas mark 6.

Spread about a tablespoon of the asparagus purée in the middle of each tart. Arrange the asparagus tips on top of the purée and intersperse with pieces of goat's cheese. Season. Bake the tarts for 8 minutes and serve immediately.

STEAMED WHITE ASPARAGUS WITH CREAMED MORELS

A classic spring dish, with the first morels and white asparagus arriving at J Sheekey in April from France. The freshness of both is paramount here, so search out your finest supplier.

SERVES 4

FRESH MORELS	100g, halved
UNSALTED BUTTER	30g
SHALLOTS	2, peeled and finely chopped
WHITE WINE	50ml
DOUBLE CREAM	250ml
SALT AND FRESHLY GROUND BLACK PEPPER	
FRESHLY GRATED PARMESAN	2 tbsp
TARRAGON	½ small bunch, chopped
WHITE ASPARAGUS	20 medium
CASTER SUGAR	½ tbsp
LEMON	½, juiced

Morels can be a bit gritty due to their honeycombed texture, so wash them a couple of times in cold water, drain and pat dry on kitchen paper.

In a heavy-bottomed saucepan, melt the butter and gently cook the shallots and morels for about 5 minutes until soft. Add the white wine and reduce by half. Add double cream, season and bring to the boil. Simmer on a low heat until the sauce has reduced by half and thickened. Add the Parmesan and tarragon and set aside.

Meanwhile, cut about 3cm off the base of the asparagus (if woody cut a little more). Using a peeler, carefully peel the stalks, starting from 3cm down from the tip.

Bring a saucepan of salted water to the boil with the sugar and the lemon juice. Simmer the asparagus for 10 to 15 minutes until the spears are tender. Carefully drain in a colander and arrange on plates.

To serve, gently re-heat the creamed morels and spoon over the tips of the asparagus.

Adding a little sugar and lemon juice to water when cooking white asparagus gives it a slightly sweet, yet savoury flavour.

COD TONGUES WITH CEPS AND BONE MARROW

Gelatinous in texture and deliciously sweet in flavour, we first came across *langues de cabillaud* fifteen years ago in the fish market in Boulogne and later found reference to them as 'cod tongues' in *Jane Grigson's Fish Cookery*. We source ours from Scandinavia. You may find cod tongues difficult to come by, so order them in advance from your fishmonger.

SERVES 4

EXTRA VIRGIN OLIVE OIL	2 tbsp
COD TONGUES	300g
PLAIN FLOUR	For dusting
CEPS OR OTHER WILD MUSHROOMS	100g, thinly sliced
BONE MARROW	80g, diced (pre-order this from your butcher, asking for the marrow to be removed from the bones)
FLAT LEAF PARSLEY	½ small bunch, chopped
SALT AND FRESHLY GROUND BLACK PEPPER	

FOR THE SAUCE

EXTRA VIRGIN OLIVE OIL	2 tbsp
SHALLOTS	2, finely chopped
GARLIC	1 clove, peeled and crushed
THYME	2 sprigs, leaves removed and chopped
RED WINE	125ml
BEEF STOCK	250ml
UNSALTED BUTTER	50g, diced

For the sauce, heat the olive oil in a heavy-bottomed saucepan and gently cook the shallots, garlic and thyme until soft, without allowing to colour. Slowly add red wine and reduce down by two thirds. Add beef stock (a good quality cube is fine) and reduce again by two thirds. This should take about 15 minutes. To finish, whisk in diced unsalted butter to create a smooth, silky sauce. Keep warm.

Meanwhile, heat the olive oil in a non-stick frying pan. Dust the cod tongues in flour, season and fry till golden brown. Add ceps, toss together and cook for a further 2 minutes.

Stir the diced bone marrow into the cod tongue mixture, followed by the sauce and chopped parsley. Bring to the boil, season to taste and serve immediately with crusty bread.

> Wild mushrooms are best cleaned with a fine brush. If you feel the need to wash them, always keep them whole, dip them in and out of water to remove excess dirt and drain well on kitchen paper. Otherwise, they soak up water and lose their flavour.

CREAMED SALT COD, POACHED EGG AND GARLIC TOAST

Salt cod is a staple in Mediterranean countries – particularly Portugal, Spain and southern France. It can be found in the UK in many delis and supermarkets, especially during Lent. We make our own, using cod belly and tail, but here we advise using fillet.

SERVES 4–6

COD FILLET	600g, skin off and pin-boned
ROCK SALT	Up to 500g
MILK	450ml
FLOURY POTATOES	500g, peeled, cooked and dry mashed
EXTRA VIRGIN OLIVE OIL	120ml
GARLIC	4 cloves, peeled and crushed
FLAT LEAF PARSLEY	1 small bunch, finely chopped
DOUBLE CREAM	50ml
GROUND WHITE PEPPER	
CHILLI GARLIC BUTTER (*SEE PAGE 60*)	40g
BAGUETTE	1

FOR THE POACHED EGGS

FREE RANGE EGGS	4 medium
WHITE WINE VINEGAR	1 tbsp

Allow 3 days for the preparation of the salt cod. Place the cod into a large dish, cover with salt, wrap in Clingfilm and leave in the fridge for up to 2 days. After 2 days, remove the salt and run the cod under cold water for 10 minutes. Soak in water in the fridge for 12 hours. After this, rinse the cod well and pat dry with kitchen roll.

Put the cod into a saucepan, cover with milk, bring to the boil and simmer for 5 minutes. Drain in a colander and keep the cooking liquor, ensuring no bones remain.

Pre-heat the oven to 200°C / gas mark 6. Place olive oil, garlic and parsley into a small saucepan, heat (do not boil), and keep warm. In a large bowl, gently mix the mashed potato with half the cod. Add the olive oil mixture, gradually pour in the cooking liquor and cream until the consistency is like creamed mashed potato. Fold in the remaining salt cod flakes by hand. Season with a little pepper. Divide the mixture into small earthenware dishes, place in the oven and cook for 20 minutes.

While this is cooking, thinly slice the baguette at an angle. Place on a baking tray. Melt the garlic butter and pour over the bread. Place into the oven and cook until golden brown.

Poach the eggs, see page 94.

Take the cod dishes out of the oven. Place the poached eggs on top of the salt cod and serve with garlic toast.

HOW TO PREPARE SQUID

1   Gently remove the tentacles from the body, taking the insides with them.

2   Cut the tentacles away from the body just below the eye. Keep the tentacles and discard the rest.

3   Squeeze the tentacles, remove the beak and discard.

4   Reach into the main body of the squid and remove the clear plastic-like quill. Discard.

5 Gently pull the 2 wings from the body, and keep.

6 Peel off the coloured membrane.

7 Slit the squid down one side to open it up and, using the back of a knife, scrape away any contents that are left. Rinse under running cold water.

8 Gently score the inside of the squid taking care not to cut too deeply.

GRILLED SQUID, SLOW-COOKED TOMATOES, PANCETTA AND ROCKET

SERVES 4

EXTRA VIRGIN OLIVE OIL	75ml
PANCETTA	25g, diced
SMOKED PAPRIKA	¼ tsp
GARLIC	2 cloves, peeled and crushed
OREGANO OR MARJORAM	2 sprigs
CHERRY VINE TOMATOES	200g, cut in half
SPRING ONIONS	½ bunch, thinly diced
SQUID	400g, cleaned
SALT AND FRESHLY GROUND BLACK PEPPER	
ROCKET	100g, picked and washed
LEMON	1, juiced

First prepare your squid (see page 126). Heat some of the olive oil in a frying pan, add the pancetta and cook gently until golden brown. Add the smoked paprika, garlic, oregano or marjoram and tomatoes and cook gently until the tomatoes soften. Add the spring onion and stir well. Remove from the heat and leave to one side.

Heat a ribbed griddle pan until it's smoking. Season the squid with salt, pepper and oil. Grill for a minute or so on each side. Any longer and it will toughen. The flesh should have charred stripes from the pan. Remove and cut into large strips.

Arrange the tomato mixture on 4 plates. Place the squid on top and finish with rocket leaves tossed in lemon juice and olive oil.

Place a heat-resistant object (such as a small baking dish or lid) on top of the squid to prevent it from curling at the sides – being careful not to burn yourself when you remove it.

RISOTTO NERO WITH SAUTÉED SQUID

A delicately flavoured silky dish in contrast to its dramatic appearance. In the Veneto region of Italy, they more commonly use cuttlefish. This is a classic dish at our sister restaurant Le Caprice.

SERVES 4

EXTRA VIRGIN OLIVE OIL	2 tbsp
SHALLOT	1, peeled and finely diced
THYME	1 sprig
GARLIC	1 clove, peeled and crushed
CARNAROLI RICE	200g
SQUID INK	50g
WHITE WINE	125ml
FISH STOCK	1 litre
UNSALTED BUTTER	30g, cold and diced
SQUID	200g, cleaned and diced (see page 126)
FLAT LEAF PARSLEY	1 small bunch, chopped
SALT AND FRESHLY GROUND BLACK PEPPER	

For the risotto, heat a tablespoon of olive oil in a heavy-bottomed saucepan, add the shallot, thyme and garlic and stir on a low heat for a couple of minutes, without allowing to colour. Add the rice and cook for a couple of minutes on a low heat.

Next add the squid ink and stir in well. Increase the heat and add the white wine, allowing it to bubble and reduce by about half. Slowly add the stock (see page 37, but a good quality cube is fine), a ladle or two at a time, stirring constantly and ensuring all the liquid has been absorbed before adding more. This process shouldn't take more than 20 minutes.

When the rice is cooked, stir in the butter and a little more stock if needed. The risotto should be wet, but not runny.

Meanwhile, in a frying pan, add a tablespoon of olive oil and fry the squid until golden brown. Add the chopped parsley and season.

Spoon the risotto into bowls, scatter the squid over it and serve immediately.

MAINS

ROASTED BRILL ON THE BONE WITH WILD GARLIC MASH AND ST GEORGE'S MUSHROOMS

Revered in France as *le mousseron vrai*, 'the true mousseron', the season for St George's mushrooms *Calocybe gambosa*, traditionally starts on 23 April, St George's Day, though they are more likely to be found through May. Loved by our chefs for their firm texture and creamy, woody flavour, they often grow in abundant (fairy) rings in pasture, verges and woodland edges. Warning: as with all wild mushrooms, please be extremely careful as St George's are easily confused with poisonous varieties. It is safer to order, as we do, from a specialist supplier. Wild garlic is readily available in the UK from March until the end of May.

SERVES 4

BRILL	1 large, cut into 4 on the bone
ST GEORGE'S MUSHROOMS (*OR OTHER SEASONAL WILD MUSHROOM*)	150g
SHALLOT	1 small, finely chopped
SUNFLOWER OIL	For frying
UNSALTED BUTTER	60g
LEMON	½, juiced
CHIVES	½ small bunch, chopped
SALT AND FRESHLY GROUND BLACK PEPPER	

FOR THE WILD GARLIC MASH

WILD GARLIC	Large handful, chopped
UNSALTED BUTTER	30g
MILK	100ml
DOUBLE CREAM	50ml
KING EDWARD POTATOES	500g
SALT AND GROUND WHITE PEPPER	

To make the mash, boil the potatoes in a saucepan of salted water for 20 minutes or until soft, and drain well. Mash in the pan until smooth or put through a ricer (do not use a blender!). Return to the heat, add milk and stir. Fold in the butter then cream. Finish with wild garlic, stir well, and season. Keep warm.

Heat oil in a large non-stick frying pan. Season the brill and cook for 5 minutes. Turn over for a further 5 minutes. Remove and keep warm. Wipe the pan with kitchen roll, heat oil, add the shallot and cook for 2 minutes without colour. Add St George's mushrooms, turn up the heat and cook for 4 to 5 minutes until soft. Add butter, lemon juice and chopped chives. Season.

To serve, spoon some wild garlic mash onto each plate. Place the brill on top and scatter with St George's mushrooms.

HOW TO FILLET A FLAT FISH

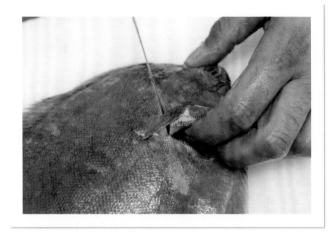

1 Place the fish on a flat surface with the dark skin facing upwards. Using a sharp, flexible, thin-bladed knife, cut around the head.

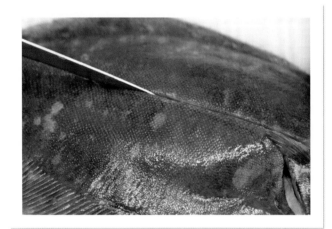

2 Run the knife down the middle of the fish from one end to the other.

3 At the head end, slide the knife under the flesh, touching the bone, and, at an angle, gently cut through to the tail.

4 Repeat on the other side.

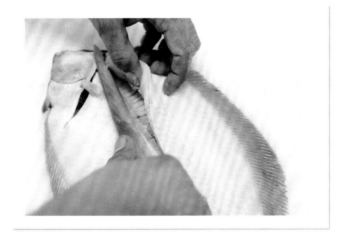

5 Turn the fish over, and repeat the process.

6 To skin the fillet, turn it flesh side up. Run the knife from the tail end as closely as possible to the skin down the full length of the fillet, holding the skin firmly whilst separating it from the flesh.

FILLET OF LEMON SOLE BELLE MEUNIÈRE

A classic dish from the days of haute cuisine that deserves revival. Sadly, many of the great dishes that appeared in Escoffier's *Le Guide Culinaire* (1903) rarely surface these days. We particularly like this combination, as the sweet brown shrimps complement the slightly bitter taste of the herring roe.

SERVES 4

SOFT HERRING ROES	250g, fresh or frozen
MILK	300ml
BAY LEAF	1
THYME	1 sprig
SUNFLOWER OIL	For frying
LEMON SOLE FILLETS	4 x 180g, skinned
PLAIN FLOUR	For dusting
BROWN SHRIMPS (OR PRAWNS)	125g, peeled and cooked
UNSALTED BUTTER	150g
FLAT LEAF PARSLEY	½ small bunch, chopped
LEMON	½, juiced
SALT AND GROUND WHITE PEPPER	

Put the herring roes in a saucepan with the milk, bay leaf, thyme and a pinch of salt. Bring to the boil and simmer for 2 minutes. Remove roes and drain on kitchen paper.

Heat oil in a non-stick frying pan. Add the lemon sole and fry for 3 minutes on each side until golden brown. Remove and keep warm.

Lightly flour the herring roes. Wipe the frying pan with kitchen roll, heat some more oil and fry the roes until golden brown. Add the brown shrimps, butter, flat leaf parsley and lemon juice. Season. This should take no more than 5 minutes.

Place the lemon sole in the middle of a warm plate. Spoon the herring roes on top and pour the shrimp and parsley butter over the top and around the fish to finish. Serve with wilted spinach (see page 182).

DOVER SOLE ON THE BONE – GRILLED OR PAN-FRIED

The quintessential British restaurant dish and always a J Sheekey bestseller. Along with turbot, this is the finest of the white fish. Fishmongers traditionally skin Dover sole on the darker top side only, leaving the white skin in place. Don't be concerned; once cooked it falls away easily from the firm flesh and bone. This dish also works very well with halibut, John Dory, plaice, lemon sole, turbot or brill.

SERVES 4

DOVER SOLE	4 x 360g, skinned
SALT AND FRESHLY GROUND BLACK PEPPER	
PLAIN FLOUR	For dusting
SUNFLOWER OIL	For frying
UNSALTED BUTTER	10g

FOR THE BÉARNAISE

HOLLANDAISE SAUCE (*SEE PAGE 116*)	250ml
TARRAGON	½ bunch, chopped
CHERVIL	½ bunch, chopped

To make the Béarnaise sauce, add the herbs to the hollandaise and mix well.

Prepare the fish by seasoning and lightly flouring them.

To pan-fry the fish, heat the oil in a non-stick frying pan and fry until golden on both sides. This should take about 6 minutes on each side.

To grill the fish, place them on a hot grill pan and cover with butter. Cook for up to 10 to 12 minutes on one side only.

To serve, place the fish onto plates with the Béarnaise sauce on the side, a fresh green vegetable and heritage potatoes.

SLIP SOLES WITH SPICED WINKLE BUTTER

Slip soles are prized on the British coast for being small, cheap and sweet to eat. Snap them up if you see them. Winkles, however, are beloved by the French (of course) and were once a staple of the British seaside, doused in vinegar and white pepper and eaten with a pin. Here they are returned to their rightful place as a tiny, briny treat. This recipe also works well with shrimps, Queenie scallops, cockles and clams.

SERVES 4

SLIP SOLES	8, skinned
SUNFLOWER OIL	For frying
SHALLOT	1 small, finely chopped
MILD CHILLI	1 medium, deseeded and finely chopped
GARLIC	1 clove, peeled and crushed
UNSALTED BUTTER	60g
LEMON	½, juiced
TARRAGON	½ small bunch, chopped
CAYENNE	Pinch
SALT AND FRESHLY GROUND BLACK PEPPER	

FOR THE WINKLES

CARROT	½, peeled and finely chopped
ONION	½ small, peeled and finely chopped
CELERY	½ stick , finely chopped
GARLIC	1 clove, peeled and crushed
BAY LEAF	1
THYME	3 sprigs
WHITE WINE VINEGAR	1 tbsp
SALT AND FRESHLY GROUND BLACK PEPPER	
FRESH WINKLES	250g

To cook the winkles, firstly place the vegetables, herbs, vinegar and seasoning into a saucepan with a litre of water, bring to the boil and simmer for 15 minutes. Add the winkles and simmer gently for 25 minutes. To check if cooked, pick one of the winkles out of its shell with a toothpick or pin. It should come out easily. Leave in the liquor to cool.

Pre-heat the oven to 180°C / gas mark 4.

When the winkles are cool, drain off the liquor and pick them out of their shells. Discard the shells and the hard 'foot'. Put the winkles in a bowl and set aside.

Season the slip soles. Heat the oil in a large non-stick frying pan (you will have to do this in batches). Add the soles and cook for 3 minutes on each side until golden brown. Remove to a warm oven.

Wipe the frying pan with kitchen roll, heat more oil and add the shallot, chilli and garlic and cook for 1 to 2 minutes without allowing them to colour. Add the winkles and toss through. Add butter, lemon juice, tarragon and Cayenne. Check seasoning. Leave the winkle butter to simmer gently for a couple of minutes.

To serve, place the slip soles on a large oval dish and spoon over the spiced winkle butter.

PLAICE WITH CRAB AND KALAMATA OLIVE STUFFING

Here, the olives add piquancy to the sweet fish. We avoid buying British plaice between December and March because it's full of roe and the flesh is soft when cooked.

SERVES 4

PLAICE FILLETS	4 x 150g, skinned
EXTRA VIRGIN OLIVE OIL	For cooking
WHITE WINE	50ml
LEMON	1, juiced

FOR THE STUFFING

UNSALTED BUTTER	50g
SHALLOT	1, finely chopped
GARLIC	1 clove, peeled and crushed
MILD CHILLI	½ medium, deseeded and finely chopped
FRESH WHITE BREADCRUMBS	100g
WHITE CRAB MEAT	100g
KALAMATA BLACK OLIVES	30g, finely chopped
FLAT LEAF PARSLEY	½ bunch, finely chopped
LEMON	1, zested
EXTRA VIRGIN OLIVE OIL	Splash
SALT AND FRESHLY GROUND BLACK PEPPER	

For the stuffing, heat the butter in a saucepan, add shallot, garlic and chilli and cook for 2 minutes until soft. Add the breadcrumbs and cook for a further minute. Remove from the heat, add crab, olives, parsley and lemon zest and mix well. If the stuffing seems dry, add a splash of olive oil and season.

Pre-heat the oven to 200°C / gas mark 6.

Place the fillets onto a clean work surface, put the stuffing in the middle of each fillet, and roll up from the tail end to the other end. This should hold perfectly well. Place each fillet into an oven-proof baking dish. Splash the olive oil, lemon juice and white wine over the fish and bake for 15 minutes.

Serve with wilted spinach and buttered potatoes.

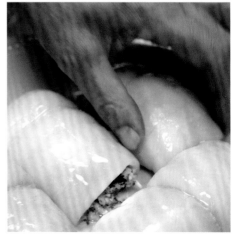

ROAST POLLACK WITH SCAMPI PROVENÇAL

'The anti-pollack brigade are the fishy equivalent of flat-earthists and it's time they were stopped.' So says Fish Fight champion Hugh Fearnley-Whittingstall, and, while we perhaps wouldn't go that far, it's true to say it's taking time for the UK consumer to appreciate this fine member of the cod family, still abundant in British waters. Ignore the naming issues (a couple of years ago a leading supermarket renamed it 'Colin' to avoid embarrassment!), join in the Fish Fight, and treat yourself to this dish.

SERVES 4

SUNFLOWER OIL	For frying
LANGOUSTINE TAILS	160g, shelled
POLLACK FILLETS	4 x 180g

FOR THE PROVENÇAL SAUCE

EXTRA VIRGIN OLIVE OIL	60ml
SHALLOTS	2, peeled and finely chopped
GARLIC	4 cloves, peeled and crushed
THYME	3 sprigs, chopped
OREGANO OR MARJORAM	3 sprigs, chopped
ROSEMARY	3 sprigs, chopped
TOMATO PUREE	2 tbsp
WHITE WINE	125ml
PLUM TOMATOES	12, peeled, deseeded and roughly chopped into 1½cm chunks
SALT AND FRESHLY GROUND BLACK PEPPER	

For the provençal sauce, heat olive oil in a heavy-bottomed saucepan and gently cook the shallots, garlic and herbs for 5 minutes until soft, being careful not to let them colour. Stir in the tomato purée and cook for a minute. Add the white wine and simmer until it has almost completely reduced. Add the plum tomatoes, season and cook for 10 minutes. Set aside and re-season if necessary.

Heat the sunflower oil in a non-stick frying pan and fry the langoustine tails on a high heat for about 2 minutes until golden brown. Remove from the frying pan and add to the provençal sauce.

Season the pollack. Wipe the frying pan with kitchen roll and add more oil. Gently cook the fish, skin-side down, for 5 minutes. Turn over for a further 4 minutes.

Re-heat the provençal sauce in a saucepan. Spoon onto warm plates, with the pollack on top. Serve with rice.

JOHN DORY WITH ROASTED CHERRY VINE TOMATOES, BARBA DI FRATE AND CAPERS

Barba di Frate or monk's beard (or goat's beard) is named after the Italian Cappuccino monks who cultivated it, and has a limited season in early spring. Still coming mostly from the Mediterranean region, it is increasingly grown here by specialist suppliers. Use samphire or asparagus if you cannot track it down.

SERVES 4

CHERRY VINE TOMATOES	400g
GARLIC	1 clove, peeled and crushed
EXTRA VIRGIN OLIVE OIL	50ml
THYME	2 sprigs, chopped
SEA SALT	1 tsp
CASTER SUGAR	Pinch
SALT AND FRESHLY GROUND BLACK PEPPER	
MONK'S BEARD	200g
CAPERS	20g
LEMON	½, zested and juiced
JOHN DORY FILLETS	4 x 180g, skin on
SUNFLOWER OIL	For frying
BASIL	½ small bunch

Pre-heat the oven to 190ºC / gas mark 5.

Remove the cherry tomatoes from the vine, halve them and lay, cut-side up, on a baking tray. Mix garlic, olive oil, thyme, sea salt, sugar and black pepper and brush or spoon over the tomatoes. Cook in the oven for about 10 to 15 minutes until the tomatoes start to blister. Remove from the oven, put them in a mixing bowl and leave to cool, ensuring you retain the cooking juices for the dressing.

Bring a saucepan of salted water to the boil and blanch the monk's beard for a minute. It should be crunchy when you remove it from the water. Drain in a colander, plunge into cold water and drain again. Add monk's beard, capers, lemon juice and zest to the tomatoes, mix well, and season to taste.

Heat the sunflower oil in a non-stick frying pan. Season the John Dory fillets and gently cook, skin–side down, for 4 minutes. Turn over and cook for a further 3 minutes.

To serve, place the tomato and monk's beard mix onto a large oval serving dish. Place the fish on top and garnish with basil leaves. We serve this with buttered Jersey Royals.

FISH AND CHIPS

MOST POPULAR FISH WITH CHIPS:

Cod 61.5%

Haddock 25%

Others (including hake, halibut, huss, plaice, sole) 13.5%

Source: seafish.org

The country's favourite fast food, a blend of Jewish and Huguenot cultures spread through the UK by Italian migrants, the rise (and fall) of fish and chips is British culture on a plate – or wrapped in paper. But first, some facts and figures. The British eat three million servings a year, mostly from around 10,000 'chippies' (down from 35,000 in 1929). They were exempted from rationing in World War II as an essential foodstuff. Winston Churchill famously called them 'the good companions', and George Orwell in *The Road to Wigan Pier* (1937) put fish and chips first among the reasons the British 'averted revolution'.

The first UK recipe for 'thin cut potatoes cooked in oil' appeared in 1855 in celebrated Victorian cook Alexis Benoist Soyer's recipe book, *A Shilling Cookery Book for the People*, although, according to the Oxford English Dictionary, the earliest literary usage of 'chips' as food appears in Dickens's *A Tale of Two Cities* (1859), where the author lovingly conjures 'husky chips of potatoes, fried with some reluctant drops of oil'. Dickens also writes of a 'fried fish warehouse' in *Oliver Twist* in 1838, although here the fish would have come with bread or a baked potato and been introduced by Jewish refugees from Portugal and Spain. Chips were introduced to the UK by Huguenots who had fled persecution to work in silk and lace around the Spitalfields area of east London, although a blue plaque marks the country's first chip shop in Tommyfield Market, Oldham.

It is here the facts become confused between rival claims from north and south. Some say credit for first selling 'fish 'n' chips' goes to trader John Lees, who operated out of a hut in Mossley Market in Lancashire in 1863. Others argue the first shop was opened by a Jewish immigrant, Joseph Malin, near Bow Bells around 1860. But what is known is that it was Italian migrants who set up shop throughout the UK, wrapping portions in old newspaper to keep costs down. This survived into the 1980s when it was ruled unsafe, but what still stands is the practice that fish is sold by species: 'cod and chips' not 'fish and chips', or more likely, 'jumbo haddock' fried in beef dripping if you are from the old coal-mining and woollen-manufacturing districts of West Yorkshire.

The first fish 'n' chip restaurant was opened in London in 1896 by wholesaler Samuel Isaacs of Whitechapel, serving fish and chips, bread and butter, and tea for nine pence (about 3p) with waitered service, tablecloths, flowers, china and cutlery, making it the first 'restaurant' experience for many working people. J Sheekey opened in London's theatre district in the same year but were forbidden at first to fry fish by a lease limiting them to serving 'boiled' (steamed) or grilled fish for the cultured classes. Now, of course, these boundaries between parts of the country and class are mostly gone, and J Sheekey's celebrated haddock, chips and mushy peas are rightly recognised as among the finest found on these shores. Our chefs' secret recipe appears overleaf.

  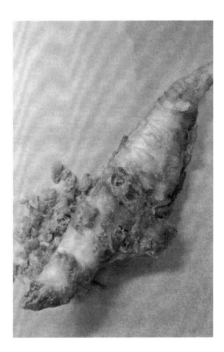

FISH AND CHIPS AND MINTED MUSHY PEAS

This is our version of traditional British seaside fish 'n' chips and mushy peas. Traditionally, fish that deep fry well include cod, haddock and plaice, though in the UK, which fish to use and whether you prefer to fry in beef dripping or oil will largely depend on where you live and where you were brought up. Oily fish, such as red mullet and mackerel, are not recommended. We favour haddock cooked in oil.

SERVES 4

HADDOCK	4 x 170g
SALT AND FRESHLY GROUND BLACK PEPPER	
PLAIN FLOUR	50g

FOR THE BATTER

LAGER	330ml
SELF-RAISING FLOUR	160g
CAYENNE	Pinch
SOY SAUCE	Dash
SALT AND GROUND WHITE PEPPER	

FOR THE MINTED MUSHY PEAS

UNSALTED BUTTER	50g
ONION	1 small, finely chopped
PEAS	500g, shelled or frozen
VEGETABLE STOCK	100ml
MINT	½ small bunch
SALT AND FRESHLY GROUND BLACK PEPPER	

FOR THE CHIPS

MARIS PIPER POTATOES	1kg
SUNFLOWER OIL	For frying
SALT	

For the batter, pour the beer into a large mixing bowl and gently whisk in the flour until you get a smooth and silky consistency (you may need to add more or less flour). Add Cayenne, soy sauce and seasoning. Leave in the fridge till ready to use. This can be made an hour before needed.

To prepare the peas, heat half the butter in a saucepan and gently cook the onion until soft but not coloured. Add the peas, vegetable stock (see page 70, but a good quality cube is fine) and mint leaves and simmer for 10 minutes. Blend in a food processor, taking care to prevent it from becoming too smooth. Season. You can also prepare this in advance. Just before serving, re-heat the peas and stir in the remaining butter.

For the chips, peel the potatoes and cut chips 1½cm wide and 7cm long. Wash the chips in water, drain on kitchen paper and pat dry. Pour the oil into a heavy-bottomed saucepan or deep fat fryer. Heat to 120°C. If using a heavy-bottomed saucepan, please be careful as the oil will be very hot. Blanch the chips, 2 or 3 handfuls at a time, until they are soft but not coloured. You can test them with a knife by carefully removing one whilst cooking to see if it is soft. Once ready, remove and drain.

Turn up the deep fat fryer to 160°C. Season and lightly flour the fish, dip into the batter and fry in the hot fat. This will take about 8 minutes. Drain and keep warm. Re-fry the chips until crisp. Season lightly with salt. Spoon the minted mushy peas onto plates, place the fish on top and serve chips on the side.

ICONIC COD

The nose-to-tail fish

MOUTH-WATERING smoked cod roe on toast with horseradish butter; cheeks and samphire with tartare sauce; tongues with ceps and bone marrow; creamed salt cod, poached egg and garlic toast; chitterlings with ravigote sauce; filleted with cockles, sea purslane and parsley; with braised lentils and prosciutto; and the fabled dish that always flies off the menu: cod and crushed potatoes with lobster and tarragon. Just a few of the recipes that appear on these pages. Some J Sheekey chefs call cod the 'pork of the sea', a professional cook's homage to its 'nose-to-tail' quality. Much like the Italians use every part of the pig, it is the most versatile fish in the restaurant repertoire.

Cod – fish of the genus *Gadus*, belonging to the *gadidae* family – has been an international commodity for more than 1,000 years, since ninth-century Norwegians sold it dried as stockfish and later as salt cod to the southern Mediterranean countries where it is still central to their diet. Its once breathtaking abundance (mankind still consumes about 40 billion lb of 'cod-like' fish every year!) fed the expansion of the 'old' world and was integral to the discovery of the 'new'.

Vikings, Portuguese, French and English boats all fished the waters of the northwest Atlantic, and Basque fishermen are said to have stumbled on America centuries before Columbus in search of cod, but kept it secret in order to avoid sharing their fishing grounds. Five years after Columbus, in 1497 the crew of John Cabot's voyage wrote of the sea there being so 'full of fish that can be taken not only with nets but with fishing-baskets'. A hundred years later, English captains were still writing of shoals 'so thick by the shore that we hardly have been able to row a boat through them'.

The abundance would last until the mid twentieth century and the arrival of factory fishing. Massive modern trawlers with on-board freezing facilities were soon plundering stocks on an industrial scale, taking near to half a million tons a year from Newfoundland waters and 800,000 tons from Canada's Grand Banks. In a scant fifteen years they fished more than the previous hundred. Of course, it couldn't last. By 1974 the Grand Banks catch had dived to a catastrophic 34,000 tons.

The collapse forced the debate on sustainable fishing and governments to act. The once-teeming banks were shut to commercial fishing in 1994 and designated 'boxes' (controlled areas) were created where fish could be caught. Now, decades later, there are hesitant signs for optimism, cod is creeping back, appearing again off Cape Cod, Canada, even Cornwall, although not yet at the same size or near to pre-collapse numbers.

Whereas a few years ago, J Sheekey seriously considered taking it off their menu, their work with a number of carefully vetted and trusted suppliers, fishing responsibly from sustainable sources, means this iconic fish is again available in all its versatile glory.

With its beautifully subdued green-dappled skin and translucent, flaky white flesh, cod deserves our respect, and its place as the world's best loved fish. We are proud of the recipes overleaf and commend them to you, but please be sure to ask your fishmonger about their own sustainable supplies.

COD WITH COCKLES, SEA PURSLANE AND PARSLEY

Sea purslane grows in salt marsh on much of the coastline of England and Wales. If foraging, take the top leaves from plants on higher ground as too much time under water toughens the leaves. It is abundant and available throughout the year but please be sensitive to overcropping in one area. For anyone not near the coast, it is available from specialist suppliers. We also use sea purslane with grilled shellfish. For more about gathering sea purslane and samphire, see page 162.

SERVES 4

EXTRA VIRGIN OLIVE OIL	1 tbsp
COD FILLETS	4 x 180g
SALT AND FRESHLY GROUND BLACK PEPPER	
COCKLES	350g
WHITE WINE	125ml
BLANCHED SEA PURSLANE OR OTHER SEA VEGETABLE (*SAMPHIRE IN SEASON IS PERFECT*)	80g
UNSALTED BUTTER	100g
DOUBLE CREAM	80ml
FLAT LEAF PARSLEY	Small bunch, finely chopped
LEMON	Squeeze

Heat a non-stick frying pan. Add olive oil. Season the cod fillets and gently cook skin-side down for 5 minutes. Turn over and cook for a further 4 minutes.

While the cod is cooking, heat a heavy-bottomed saucepan. Add the cockles and white wine, and cover. Toss gently until shells begin to open, which should happen after about 4 minutes. Drain off a little of the liquid, add the sea purslane, butter and cream, and stir. Bring to the boil, add the parsley, a squeeze of lemon and check the seasoning.

Place the cod on warm plates and arrange the cockles and sea purslane over and around the fish.

COD WITH BRAISED LENTILS AND PROSCIUTTO

Prosciutto or bacon is the perfect accompaniment to pulses. This is a great winter dish when cod is eaten at its best.

SERVES 4

PROSCIUTTO	4 thin slices
SUNFLOWER OIL	For frying
COD FILLETS	4 x 180g
SALT AND FRESHLY GROUND BLACK PEPPER	

FOR THE LENTILS

PUY LENTILS	250g
EXTRA VIRGIN OLIVE OIL	40ml
THICK PROSCIUTTO	100g, diced (ask your deli for the end of the ham or use cubes of pancetta)
ONION	1, finely diced
CARROT	1, finely diced
LEEK	1, finely diced and washed
CELERY	1 stick, finely diced
GARLIC	2 cloves, peeled and crushed
THYME	2 sprigs, leaves removed and chopped
ROSEMARY	2 sprigs, leaves removed and chopped
CHICKEN STOCK	1 litre
UNSALTED BUTTER	30g
FLAT LEAF PARSLEY	½ small bunch, finely chopped
SALT AND FRESHLY GROUND BLACK PEPPER	

Start preparing the lentils by soaking them in cold water for an hour.

Pre-heat the oven to 160°C / gas mark 3. Spread the thin prosciutto out onto a baking dish and cook in the oven until crisp. This should take around 20 minutes, but keep a watchful eye so that it doesn't dry out too much. Keep to one side.

Pour 20ml olive oil into a heavy-bottomed saucepan and gently cook the thick prosciutto, onion, carrot, leek, celery, garlic, thyme and rosemary for 5 minutes. Add the drained lentils, stir, and then add the chicken stock (a good quality cube is fine). Bring to the boil and simmer until the lentils are soft to taste, but not mushy. This should take around 20 minutes, but taste to check. The consistency should be sauce-like. Set aside.

Heat a non-stick frying pan. Add the sunflower oil. Season the cod and gently cook skin-side down for 5 minutes. Turn over and cook for a further 4 minutes.

To serve, re-heat the lentils and gently stir in the butter and parsley, and season. Spoon the lentils onto warm plates, place the cod on top and garnish with the crispy prosciutto.

COD AND CRUSHED POTATOES WITH LOBSTER AND TARRAGON

This dish has been on the menu as long as our records go back. The addition of lobster elevates the humble potato here into an enduring favourite, although it is also delicious with prawns.

SERVES 4

LOBSTER	1 x 500g, cooked (see page 48)
WAXY POTATOES	250g small, peeled
TARRAGON	½ bunch, stalks retained, leaves chopped
UNSALTED BUTTER	40g
SALT AND FRESHLY GROUND BLACK PEPPER	
SUNFLOWER OIL	For frying
COD FILLETS	4 x 180g

FOR THE LOBSTER SAUCE

EXTRA VIRGIN OLIVE OIL	For frying lobster shells (see method)
SHALLOT	1, roughly chopped
CARROT	½, peeled and finely diced
CELERY	½ stalk, finely diced
GARLIC	1 clove, peeled and crushed
TARRAGON STALKS (*SEE ABOVE*)	½ bunch
TOMATO PUREE	1 tbsp
UNSALTED BUTTER	20g
PLAIN FLOUR	2 tbsp
WHITE WINE	100ml
FISH STOCK	200ml, kept hot in a saucepan
DOUBLE CREAM	50ml
SALT AND FRESHLY GROUND BLACK PEPPER	

Remove lobster meat from the shells (retaining shells for the sauce). Chop into smallish pieces and set aside.

For the sauce, pour the olive oil into a large heavy-bottomed saucepan and fry the lobster shells, shallot, carrot, celery and garlic over a medium heat for about 5 minutes, until they begin to colour lightly. Stir in the tarragon stalks and tomato purée and combine well. Add butter and allow it to melt. Add the flour, stirring well. Slowly add the white wine and fish stock (see page 37, but a good quality cube is fine), stirring continuously to avoid lumps. Bring to the boil and simmer for about 20 minutes until the sauce has reduced by half.

Add the cream to the sauce and stir well. Bring to the boil and simmer gently for about 15 minutes, until the sauce has reduced by half and has a thick consistency. Strain through a sieve into a bowl, pressing down with the back of a spoon to extract all the liquid. Check seasoning and keep warm.

Cook the potatoes in boiling salted water until just tender, drain and dry off in the hot pan. Crush the potatoes with a fork and mix with the lobster meat, tarragon leaves and 4 tablespoons of lobster sauce. Add butter, season and heat slowly, stirring every so often. Cover and keep warm.

Heat a non-stick frying pan. Add sunflower oil. Season the cod and gently cook skin-side down for 5 minutes. Turn over and cook for a further 4 minutes.

Spoon the mash onto the centre of each plate, place the fish on top, skin-side up. Re-heat the sauce and pour round the fish.

SEA VEGETABLES ✳ FORAGER ✳ KENT ✳

For maybe the tenth time today we stop on our coastal walk, near Graveney in Kent. Miles Irving grins, stops, stoops and takes out his knife. The small, shy plant hidden in among the marsh grass we could, would, have missed, is lovingly exposed, cut and lifted. He gently pares back the leaves. 'You can see why they call it buck's horn plantain,' he says as he hands us an antler-shaped frond. And for the tenth time today we experience a new taste as its subdued, salty flavours flood into our mouth. To many, it's just another anonymous weed but to Irving, and to the J Sheekey chefs, it is food from the wild British coast, adding depth and texture to a briny broth with clams.

1

2

Irving, a professional forager with a catalogue of around 120 edible plants, fruits and fungus, has been supplying a range of seasonal wild foods and flavours – including cobnuts, wood sorrel, wild garlic, elderflower and berries, sea beet, sea purslane, sea aster and samphire – to J Sheekey for seven years, since he first started. Ask him his favourite 'found food' and he will tell you it's wild celery because he 'can feel its benefits in his arms and legs only moments after eating it'. His second favourite? Wild cabbage found on coastal cliffs. 'It is the mother plant,' he says, 'the one from which all the brassicas come, be they kale or cauliflower.'

Although the majority of Irving's business consists of coastal herbs, it is hunting for fungus that he believes is the real test of a forager. 'They are elusive,' he says, 'true hunter-gatherer food.' It takes a lot of skill to identify and find fungus and the sites they'll

grow. 'And they are the nearest I will come to a "kill".'

He has been known to stay out till 2am he says, to fill an order for ceps in summer or St George's mushrooms in spring. Irving is evangelical about found food and practises what he preaches. His breakfast most days consists of bitter dandelions from the garden, raw or cooked with his bacon and egg.

The sea wind had picked up, the cold rain is English, heavy and horizontal. Our wellingtons have survived getting sucked into the mud. We have found perennial and marsh samphire, sea blight, sea arrowgrass, sea purslane, sea lavender, which we have been eating raw, like salted crisps and peanuts. Our pockets are stuffed with wild food for the pot, our hunter-gatherer ancestors would be proud. We call it a day and switch our thoughts to hunting out a dry spot, a good saucepan and clams.

1: *Foraging*
2: *Samphire*
3: *Sea purslane*

DEEP FRIED COD CHEEKS AND SAMPHIRE WITH TARTARE SAUCE

Cod cheeks were traditionally kept back and eaten by trawlermen as a 'fisherman's friend'. Widely available in New England, their popularity here coincided with the rise of the 'gastro pub' and 'Modern British' restaurants looking to revive cheaper cuts. You may need to order them from your fishmonger.

SERVES 4

SUNFLOWER OIL	For frying
COD CHEEKS	600g
PLAIN FLOUR	For dusting
FREE RANGE EGG	1 medium, beaten
FRESH WHITE BREADCRUMBS	100g
SALT AND GROUND WHITE PEPPER	
SAMPHIRE	100g
LEMON	1

FOR THE TARTARE SAUCE

MAYONNAISE (*SEE PAGE 56*)	150ml
CORNICHONS	30g, finely chopped
CAPERS	30g
SHALLOT	1, peeled and finely chopped
FLAT LEAF PARSLEY	½ small bunch, finely chopped
LEMON	½, juiced
SALT AND FRESHLY GROUND BLACK PEPPER	

Firstly make the tartare sauce. Fold all the ingredients together and season.

Then prepare the cod cheeks. Pour 6cm of oil into a heavy-bottomed saucepan or a deep fat fryer. Heat to 160°C. If using a saucepan, please be careful as the oil will be very hot.

Season the cheeks. Dip them into the flour, then egg, then breadcrumbs. Fry in the hot oil until golden brown. Remove with tongs onto kitchen paper to soak up excess oil. Season.

Meanwhile, bring a saucepan of unsalted water to the boil and blanch the samphire for 1 minute. Strain in a colander and keep warm.

Place the cod cheeks on a large serving platter and scatter the samphire over the top. Serve with tartare sauce and lemon wedges.

SHRIMP AND SCALLOP BURGER

For when you want to eat with your hands (though here, of course, it is optional), this is our take on fish in a bun developed by our former Head Chef, Richard Kirkwood.

SERVES 4

FOR THE BURGER

SALMON FILLET	50g, skinned and chopped
RAW TIGER PRAWN TAILS	350g, ½ chopped, ½ blended
SCALLOPS	100g, without corals, chopped
SPRING ONIONS	3, thinly sliced
MILD CHILLI	3 medium, deseeded and finely chopped
FLAT LEAF PARSLEY	½ bunch, finely chopped
LEMON	½, juiced
TABASCO	Dash
SALT AND FRESHLY GROUND BLACK PEPPER	
SUNFLOWER OLIVE OIL	For frying
BURGER BUNS	4, toasted
GHERKINS	To serve

FOR THE CHILLI MAYONNAISE

MILD RED CHILLI	1 medium, deseeded and finely chopped
EXTRA VIRGIN OLIVE OIL	1 tbsp
MAYONNAISE (*SEE PAGE 56*)	150ml
FLAT LEAF PARSLEY	2 tbsp, finely chopped
LEMON	½, juiced
SALT AND FRESHLY GROUND BLACK PEPPER	

For the chilli mayonnaise, gently cook the chilli in oil for about 4 minutes, then set aside to cool. Add to the mayonnaise along with parsley and lemon juice. Season.

Pre-heat the oven to 180°C / gas mark 4.

To make the burgers, mix the salmon, prawns, scallops, spring onions, chilli and parsley together in a bowl. Add the lemon juice and Tabasco, mix well and season. Fry a small amount of the mixture to check the seasoning is correct and adapt if necessary.

Divide the mix into 4 and shape into patties. Brush each burger with a little olive oil and fry in a non-stick pan until nicely browned on either side (the outer layer will slightly caramelise). Continue cooking the burgers in the oven for 3 to 5 minutes, depending on thickness.

Serve on a toasted bun with chilli mayonnaise, gherkins and relish.

BURGER RELISH

FOR THE LIQUOR

CASTER SUGAR	1 tbsp
WHITE WINE VINEGAR	2 tsp
MUSTARD SEEDS	½ tsp
CELERY SALT (*SEE PAGE 80*)	½ tsp
WATER	2 tbsp

FOR THE VEGETABLES

RED ONION	1, finely diced
CUCUMBER	½, finely diced
CELERY	2 small stalks (from the centre), finely diced
GHERKIN	1 large, finely diced
RED PEPPER	1, finely diced
KETCHUP	90g
AMERICAN MUSTARD	90g
FRESHLY GROUND BLACK PEPPER	

Prepare the vegetables and place into a heat-proof bowl. In a saucepan, bring the ingredients for the liquor to the boil and then pour over the diced vegetables. When cool, cover with Clingfilm and leave in the refrigerator overnight.

Strain the mixture the next day and mix in the ketchup and American mustard. Season if necessary (you can add more ketchup and American mustard to taste if you like).

FISH PIE

'Merry place you may believe, Tiz Mouzel 'pon Tom Bawcock's eve
To be there then who wouldn't wesh, to sup o' sibm soorts o' fish,
When morgy brath had cleared the path, Comed lances for a fry
And then us had a bit o' scad an' Starry-gazie pie'

Traditional song from Mousehole, Cornwall

The British relationship with fish, for better or for worse, can be largely laid at the door of Rome, both the invading armies of Julius and Hadrian, etc (who appreciated fish more than us – we appear to have pretty much left it alone for 1,000 years when they left), and more importantly the Medieval Church who decreed some 200 days of fast when the eating of meat was forbidden. According to historian Helen Gaffney of the British Food Trust, it was this – including a full forty days of Lent – that forced cooks to be more inventive with fish. Pies with sugared pastries, spices and crystallised fruit (this is where mackerel and gooseberries first got together) appeared for the first time. Gervase Markham's *The English Huswife* (1615), containing 'the inward and outward virtues which ought to be in a complete woman', talks of cod paired with pear and candied lemon peel.

Then, as now, what went in your pie was dictated by local taste and availability. London eel pie makes an appearance in Shakespeare's *Lear* and there is still an Eel Pie Island, made famous by Pete Townsend of The Who in the '60s, at Twickenham. Scottish cookery writer Elizabeth Craig writes of her mother's salt cod and mashed potato. In Yorkshire, herring was combined with apples and potatoes, whereas in Cornwall, herring or pilchard appear in pasties or a Mousehole stargazie pie.

Pies with salmon also have centuries of history. Helen Gaffney describes a Batalia pie from 1675 with pastry castellations, filled with salmon and prawns, and cites Elizabeth Raffald's *The Experienced Englifh Houfe-Keeper* (1769) for its recipe for a spiced salmon pie topped with sprigs of fennel. Sheekey's famous fish pie, of course, has its own long and distinguished history, and sticks to the time-honoured tradition of 'fisherman's pie' with salmon, cod and haddock and mashed potato – a superior seafaring shepherd's pie, if you will. Our chefs' secret to its recipe unfolds overleaf.

SHEEKEY'S FISH PIE

Still the bestseller on the J Sheekey menu, our fish pie is rightly as famous as some of our customers. A true theatre dish. Some people add lobster, prawns or peas to their pie. We prefer this purer version.

SERVES 4

COD FILLET (OR ANOTHER WHITE CHUNKY FISH SUCH AS HALIBUT OR MONKFISH)	200g, skinned and cut into rough 3cm chunks
SALMON FILLET	200g, skinned and cut into rough 3cm chunks
SMOKED HADDOCK FILLET	200g, skinned and cut into rough 3cm chunks
FLAT LEAF PARSLEY	½ small bunch, chopped

FOR THE SAUCE

UNSALTED BUTTER	50g
PLAIN FLOUR	50g
WHITE WINE	125ml
FISH STOCK	500ml
DOUBLE CREAM	90ml
ENGLISH MUSTARD	1 tbsp
WORCESTERSHIRE SAUCE	1 tsp
ANCHOVY ESSENCE	½ tsp
LEMON	½, juiced
SALT AND GROUND WHITE PEPPER	

FOR THE TOPPING

FLOURY POTATOES	1kg, peeled, cooked and dry mashed
UNSALTED BUTTER	50g
MILK	50ml
SALT AND GROUND WHITE PEPPER	
FRESH WHITE BREADCRUMBS	20g
FRESHLY GRATED PARMESAN	10g

To make the sauce, melt the butter in a heavy-bottomed saucepan over a low heat and gently stir in the flour. Gradually add the wine, stirring well. Slowly add the fish stock (see page 37, but a good quality cube is fine) until you have a silky smooth sauce. Bring to the boil and simmer gently for 15 minutes. To finish, add the cream and briefly bring to the boil again. Stir in mustard, Worcestershire sauce, anchovy essence and lemon juice. (Add more mustard and Worcestershire sauce if you like it spicy.) Check seasoning.

Gently fold the fish and parsley into the hot sauce, and pour into a large pie dish, leaving a space of about 3cm from the top of the dish. Leave to cool, so the topping will sit on the sauce when piped.

Pre-heat the oven to 190°C / gas mark 5.

Mix butter and milk into the mashed potato until soft enough to spread over the fish mixture. Season. Pipe or gently fork to cover the fish.

Bake the fish pie for 30 minutes. Sprinkle over the breadcrumbs and cheese, and bake for a further 10 minutes until golden.

The best all-round potatoes are King Edwards – good for mashing, roasting and frying.

DUBLIN BAY PRAWN AND CHICKEN PIE

Inspired by a Cornish Stargazie pie from Mousehole, where the pilchard or sardine heads stick out of the pastry lid. If you can't find fresh Dublin Bay prawns (langoustines), use lobster, crayfish or prawns and make the sauce in the same way.

SERVES 4–6

DUBLIN BAY PRAWNS	16–20, fresh
CHICKEN THIGHS	500g, boned and skinned, each cut into 4 pieces
FLAT LEAF PARSLEY	½ small bunch, leaves chopped
TARRAGON	½ bunch, leaves chopped
SHORT CRUST PASTRY	1kg
FREE RANGE EGG	1 medium, beaten
SALT AND GROUND WHITE PEPPER	

FOR THE DUBLIN BAY PRAWN SAUCE

SUNFLOWER OIL	For frying
DUBLIN BAY PRAWN SHELLS	(From above)
SHALLOT	1, peeled and roughly chopped
GARLIC	1 clove, peeled and roughly chopped
SAFFRON STRANDS	Pinch
TARRAGON	3 sprigs
TOMATO PUREE	1 tbsp
UNSALTED BUTTER	60g
PLAIN FLOUR	60g
WHITE WINE	60ml
CHICKEN STOCK	1 litre, kept hot in a saucepan over a medium heat
DOUBLE CREAM	400ml
SALT AND FRESHLY GROUND BLACK PEPPER	

If not using ready-made pastry, cut the cold lard into small pieces and place in a mixing bowl. Add the sieved flour, salt and baking powder and mix with your hands to a fine breadcrumb. Slowly add the water – you may not need it all – and mix to form a soft dough. Do not over mix. Wrap in Clingfilm and store in the fridge until needed. If you have any left over, freeze for another time.

Bring a saucepan of water to the boil, add the prawns and simmer for 2 minutes. Remove with a slotted spoon and plunge into cold water. Remove the meat from the shells (and claws if they are big enough). Break the shells up a little with a heavy knife and keep to one side. Keep the best heads for presentation.

In a heavy-bottomed saucepan, bring the chicken stock (a good quality cube is fine) to the boil, add the chicken thighs and poach for 5 minutes. Remove the meat from the stock, put to one side and keep the stock hot.

To make the sauce, heat the sunflower oil in a heavy-bottomed saucepan and fry the prawn shells, shallots and garlic over a medium heat for about 5 minutes until they begin to colour lightly. Add saffron, tarragon, tomato purée and stir well. Add butter and flour and stir well into the shells. Gradually stir in the white wine and the hot stock and bring to the boil. Simmer for about 10 minutes. Add cream. Season lightly, bring to the boil and simmer for a further 5 minutes, stirring from time to time to ensure that the sauce doesn't burn.

FOR SHORT CRUST PASTRY	
LARD (*STRAIGHT FROM THE REFRIGERATOR*)	250g
STRONG FLOUR	500g
SALT	1 tsp
BAKING POWDER	1 tsp
COLD WATER	250ml

Strain the sauce through a sieve into a bowl, pressing the shells with a spoon to ensure all the sauce goes through. Pour the sauce into a clean saucepan, bring to the boil. The sauce should have a thick consistency by now. If not, simmer for a little longer and then remove from the heat. Add the chicken, prawns, parsley and tarragon leaves to the sauce. Adjust the seasoning if necessary, and fill individual pie dishes, or one large one, until about 1cm from the top.

Pre-heat the oven to 200°C / gas mark 6.

When the pie mixture is cold, roll out the pastry to a thickness of 5mm and cut out a top or tops, for the pie(s). These should be about 2cm larger all the way round than the dish (or dishes). Brush the edges of the pastry with a little of the beaten egg. Lay the pastry on top, pressing the egg-washed undersides against the rim of the dish. Cut a small slit in the top of each pie to allow steam to escape and brush with beaten egg. Place the langoustine head in the middle. Leave to rest in a cool place for 30 minutes. Cook the pies for 30 minutes if individual and 40 minutes if large, until the pastry is golden.

Serve the pie with buttered greens and heritage potatoes, such as Pink Fir Apple.

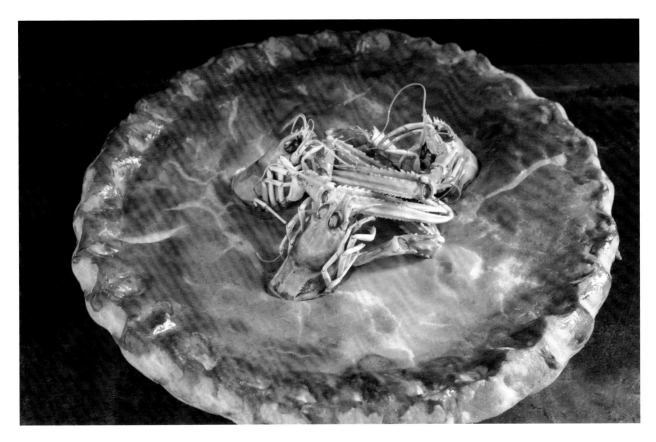

SMOKED HADDOCK WITH COLCANNON, POACHED EGG AND WHOLEGRAIN MUSTARD SAUCE

Always ask your fishmonger for naturally smoked and undyed haddock (or any other fish), with its delicate pearly, paler flesh, and avoid the inferior fish with its powder-paint bright yellow colouring. A perfect midweek supper dish.

SERVES 4

UNDYED SMOKED HADDOCK FILLETS	4 x 180g
WHITE WINE VINEGAR	Splash
FREE RANGE EGGS	4 medium

FOR THE COLCANNON

KING EDWARD POTATOES	500g
UNSALTED BUTTER	75g
SAVOY OR HISPI (POINTED) CABBAGE	½ head, finely shredded
MILK	100ml
FLAT LEAF PARSLEY	½ small bunch, chopped
SPRING ONIONS	½ bunch, finely sliced
SALT AND GROUND WHITE PEPPER	

FOR THE WHOLEGRAIN MUSTARD SAUCE
(yields approximately 200ml)

BUTTER SAUCE (*SEE PAGE 188*)	
WHOLEGRAIN MUSTARD	2 tbsp

To make the wholegrain mustard sauce, make a butter sauce (see page 188). When ready to serve, re-heat the sauce, stirring in the wholegrain mustard, being careful not to let it boil as the sauce may separate. Check seasoning.

To make the colcannon, boil the potatoes in a saucepan of salted water for 20 minutes or until soft, and drain well. Add 25g butter and mash until smooth or put through a ricer (do not use a blender!). In another saucepan, melt the rest of the butter, add the cabbage and cook slowly for 5 minutes without colour. Cover with milk, bring to the boil and add parsley and spring onions. Cook for a further 3 minutes. Stir in the mashed potato, season and keep hot.

Steam the haddock fillets, skin-side up, for 6 minutes. If you do not have a steamer, the haddock can be poached in a large saucepan filled with a mixture of half milk and half water for the same amount of time.

Poach the eggs, see page 94.

To serve, place the colcannon onto each plate with the fillet of haddock on top, removing the skin at this stage. Top with a poached egg and finish with wholegrain mustard sauce.

HALIBUT WITH CREAMED PEAS, BACON AND SCALLIONS

The largest of the coldwater flatfish, weighing up to an admittedly rare 300kg, halibut has a firm, almost meaty flesh. It can have a tendency to dry out if cooked on too high a heat or for too long, but gently heated for no more than 8 to 9 minutes, as here, it makes for a superior dish. Plus, it is fabulous for fish and chips.

SERVES 4

EXTRA VIRGIN OLIVE OIL	For frying
HALIBUT FILLETS	4 x 180g, skinned
SALT AND FRESHLY GROUND BLACK PEPPER	
LEMON	1

FOR THE CREAMED PEAS

PEAS	200g, shelled or frozen
UNSALTED BUTTER	60g
SHALLOT	1 small, finely chopped
SMOKED BACON	50g, chopped into ½cm dice
VEGETABLE STOCK	50ml
DOUBLE CREAM	120ml
SALT AND FRESHLY GROUND BLACK PEPPER	
SCALLIONS (*SPRING ONIONS*)	½ bunch, finely sliced at an angle
PEA SHOOTS OR LITTLE GEM LETTUCE	Handful, roughly shredded

Bring a saucepan of salted water to the boil, add the peas and 20g butter and cook for 5 to 6 minutes until tender (they may take more or less time, depending on size and freshness). Drain in a colander.

Meanwhile, in a larger saucepan, melt 20g butter and gently soften the shallot with the bacon, without allowing them to colour. Add the vegetable stock (see page 70, but a good quality cube is fine) and simmer until reduced by three quarters. Add the cream, season with freshly ground black pepper and simmer until reduced by half. Add peas, scallions and pea shoots or lettuce and continue to simmer until the sauce is just thick enough to coat the peas. Add the remaining butter and season if necessary. Set aside and keep warm.

Meanwhile, heat the olive oil in a non-stick frying pan. Season the halibut and gently cook for 5 minutes. Turn over and cook for a further 4 minutes.

To serve, arrange the halibut on a dish, drizzle with olive oil and garnish with lemon wedges. Place the creamed peas, bacon and scallions into a separate dish and serve with the fish, or you can serve individually with the halibut resting on a bed of the peas.

HOW TO SCALE AND FILLET ROUND FISH

1 It is usually best to ask your fishmonger to scale your salmon, sea bass, trout, sea bream etc, but if not, hold the fish by the head and run the back of a heavy knife along the skin. You will feel the scales lifting.

2 Once scaled, make an incision around the back of the head.

3 Working from the head end with a sharp, flexible, thin-bladed knife, use the back bone as a marker, and cut down the length of the fish to the tail.

4 Gently pull the flesh with your other hand. Repeat for the other side.

POACHED WILD SALMON WITH GREEN SAUCE AND MIMOSA SALAD

Wild salmon season lasts from June through to August, with its high price dropping (a little) in the middle. Eat it sparingly, ensure it was responsibly caught and savour it; it bears little resemblance to intensively farmed fish. If it is out of season or you have a limited budget, replace with organic salmon. Mimosa flowers can be made into fritters or used as a salad garnish. The name mimosa is also given to dishes using grated hard-boiled eggs mixed with mayonnaise and piped into flower shapes, or sprinkled over a mixed salad as here.

SERVES 4

FREE RANGE EGGS	2 medium
COURT BOUILLON (*SEE PAGE 50*)	1 litre
WILD SALMON FILLETS	4 x 180g, skin on
WATERCRESS	100g
LAMB'S LETTUCE	70g
SALT AND FRESHLY GROUND BLACK PEPPER	

FOR THE GREEN SAUCE

MAYONNAISE (*SEE PAGE 56*)	150ml
CREME FRAICHE	1 tbsp
FLAT LEAF PARSLEY	½ small bunch, finely chopped
TARRAGON	½ small bunch, finely chopped
CHERVIL	½ small bunch, finely chopped
CHIVES	½ small bunch, finely chopped
SALT AND FRESHLY GROUND BLACK PEPPER	

FOR THE DRESSING

WHITE WINE VINEGAR	1 tbsp
EXTRA VIRGIN OLIVE OIL	3 tbsp
EXTRA VIRGIN COLD PRESSED RAPESEED OIL	2 tbsp
LEMON	½, juiced
SALT AND FRESHLY GROUND BLACK PEPPER	

For the green sauce, mix the ingredients together in a bowl, season to taste and refrigerate until needed.

For the dressing, place all the ingredients into a jar and shake until emulsified.

Heat a saucepan of water for the eggs. When boiling, cook for 10 minutes to ensure they are hard-boiled. Cool under cold water and remove the shells.

Pour the court bouillon into a large saucepan and bring to the boil. Carefully slide the salmon fillets into the bouillon and gently simmer for 8 minutes (or 10 if you prefer your fish well done). In a salad bowl, toss the watercress and lamb's lettuce in the dressing. Finely grate the hard-boiled eggs over the top.

Remove the salmon from the bouillon with a slotted spoon and place onto plates. Add a spoonful of green sauce to each plate and serve with the mimosa salad.

SALMON FISHCAKE WITH WILTED SPINACH AND SORREL SAUCE

The dish that launched a million copycat ready-meals. Some people use white fish or add smoked haddock, but we prefer to stick to salmon.

SERVES 4

ORGANIC SALMON FILLET	325g
POTATO	325g, boiled and dry mashed
TOMATO KETCHUP	1 tbsp
ANCHOVY ESSENCE	½ tbsp
WORCESTERSHIRE SAUCE	2 dashes
ENGLISH MUSTARD	½ tbsp
SALT AND FRESHLY GROUND BLACK PEPPER	
SUNFLOWER OIL	For frying
PLAIN FLOUR	For dusting

FOR THE SORREL SAUCE

FISH STOCK	300ml
UNSALTED BUTTER	25g
PLAIN FLOUR	1 tbsp
WHITE WINE	50ml
DOUBLE CREAM	100ml
SORREL LEAVES	50g fresh, shredded
SALT AND FRESHLY GROUND BLACK PEPPER	

FOR THE WILTED SPINACH

SPINACH	1kg, washed and spun dry
EXTRA VIRGIN OLIVE OIL	1 tbsp
SALT AND FRESHLY GROUND BLACK PEPPER	

First poach the salmon in salted water for 4 to 5 minutes in a large saucepan.

For the fishcakes, mix together the potato, a third of the poached salmon, ketchup, anchovy essence, Worcestershire sauce and mustard until smooth. Season. Flake the remaining salmon and fold it in gently, ensuring that you retain some chunks of fish. Mould the mixture into round cakes and refrigerate until required.

For the sauce, bring the fish stock (see page 37, but a good quality cube is fine) to the boil in a heavy-bottomed saucepan. In another, melt the butter and stir in the flour on a low heat to make a roux (paste). Stir in the wine. When it's been absorbed, slowly add stock, stirring all the while. Simmer for 20 minutes until the sauce has thickened and is smooth, taking care not to burn. Add the cream and reduce the sauce until it has a thick pouring consistency. Stir in the sorrel and season to taste. Keep warm.

Pre-heat oven to 200 °C / gas mark 6.

To cook the fishcakes, lightly flour them and fry in oil until golden coloured on both sides. Place them in the oven to cook through for 8 to 10 minutes.

Ensure the spinach is as dry as possible. Heat the oil in a large saucepan, add the spinach, lightly season and tightly cover with a lid. Cook for 2 to 3 minutes, stirring occasionally. Drain in a colander to remove excess water.

Divide the spinach between plates, place a fishcake on top, pour over the re-heated sauce and serve.

SEA TROUT WITH SUMMER VEGETABLE RISOTTO

A favourite during its late spring and summer season, when sea trout leaves the sea to spawn. It may look like a salmon, but it could as easily have matured into a brown trout if it wasn't feeling more adventurous. (Sea trout are mostly female, while brown trout are more likely male.) It has a more delicate flavour than wild salmon. The accompanying risotto would also work with asparagus, wild garlic leaves or monk's beard.

SERVES 4

SEA TROUT FILLETS	4 x 180g, pin-boned
SALT AND FRESHLY GROUND BLACK PEPPER	
EXTRA VIRGIN OLIVE OIL	For frying
LEMON	Squeeze

FOR THE SUMMER VEGETABLE RISOTTO

PEAS	60g, shelled or frozen
BROAD BEANS	100g, podded
COURGETTE	1, diced
FRENCH BEANS	60g, trimmed and cut into 1cm pieces
SPRING ONIONS	4, cut into 1cm lengths
CARNAROLI RICE	200g
VEGETABLE STOCK	1 litre, kept warm
UNSALTED BUTTER	90g
FRESHLY GRATED PARMESAN	2 tbsp
FLAT LEAF PARSLEY	¼ small bunch, chopped
MINT	¼ small bunch, chopped
SALT AND GROUND WHITE PEPPER	

Firstly pre-cook the vegetables for the risotto. If the broad beans are large, pop the skins off with your fingers. If not, they'll be fine unpeeled. Bring a saucepan of salted water to the boil. Add all the vegetables in turn until just cooked. Remove with a slotted spoon, plunge into cold water and drain. Keep to one side.

To cook the risotto, melt 30g butter in a heavy-bottomed saucepan, add the rice and stir for a minute on a low heat with a wooden spoon. Gradually add the warm stock (see page 70, but a good quality cube is fine), a little at a time, stirring constantly and ensuring each addition of liquid has been fully absorbed before adding the next.

Season the sea trout. About 10 minutes after starting the risotto, heat a non-stick frying pan. Add a splash of olive oil and cook the sea trout, skin-side down for 5 minutes. Turn over and cook for a further 3 to 4 minutes. Remove the fish from the pan and keep warm. Continue to stir the risotto. When the rice is almost cooked (after about 20 minutes), add the vegetables and the rest of the butter, Parmesan and herbs. Check the seasoning and correct if necessary. The risotto should be moist and velvety, but not stodgy (you can always add more stock).

To serve, spoon the risotto immediately onto plates. Place the trout fillets on top.

HERB-ROASTED SEA TROUT WITH PINK FIR APPLE POTATO, SAMPHIRE AND ASPARAGUS SALAD

The popularity of 'growing your own' and discerning shopping have both heralded a revival of 'heritage potatoes'. We like Pink Fir Apple here for its fine nutty flavour.

SERVES 4

SEA TROUT FILLETS	4 x 180g, pin-boned and skinned
SALT AND FRESHLY GROUND BLACK PEPPER	
CHERVIL	¼ small bunch, finely chopped
DILL	¼ small bunch, finely chopped
FLAT LEAF PARSLEY	½ small bunch, finely chopped
EXTRA VIRGIN OLIVE OIL	For frying
PINK FIR APPLE POTATOES	200g
MAYONNAISE (*SEE PAGE 56*)	150ml
WHOLEGRAIN MUSTARD	1 tbsp

FOR THE SAMPHIRE AND ASPARAGUS SALAD

GREEN ASPARAGUS	250g medium, half-peeled, woody stems removed
SAMPHIRE	100g
MIXED SMALL SALAD LEAVES	100g
SALT AND FRESHLY GROUND BLACK PEPPER	

FOR THE DRESSING

RED WINE VINEGAR	1 tbsp
EXTRA VIRGIN COLD PRESSED RAPESEED OIL	2 tbsp
EXTRA VIRGIN OLIVE OIL	2 tbsp
CASTER SUGAR	Pinch
SALT AND FRESHLY GROUND BLACK PEPPER	

For the dressing, place all the ingredients into a jar and shake until emulsified.

Lightly season the sea trout. Mix the chopped herbs together in a bowl and dip one side of the trout into them. Heat the oil in a non-stick frying pan. Add the trout fillets, herb-side down, and cook for about 3 minutes on each side. Remove from the frying pan and set aside.

Meanwhile, bring a saucepan of salted water to the boil and cook the potatoes until tender. This should take around 15 minutes. Strain in a colander, return the potatoes to the saucepan and keep to one side. Have two further saucepans of water boiling: one salted for the asparagus and one unsalted for the samphire. Blanch the samphire for 1 minute in the unsalted water. Strain in a colander, pat dry with kitchen roll and transfer to a mixing bowl.

Slice the asparagus at an angle to around 4cm long. Cook for no more than 5 minutes or until tender – check by cutting a little off the thick end to see if the knife cuts through it easily. Drain in a colander, pat dry, and add to the samphire, along with the small salad leaves. Crush the potatoes roughly with a fork in the pan, add the mayonnaise and mustard. Season. Set aside until you're ready to serve.

Spread the crushed potatoes onto a large platter, break the trout into bite-sized pieces by hand and place on top of the potatoes. Dress the samphire and asparagus salad and arrange in between the pieces of trout.

FILLET OF RED MULLET WITH CHERVIL-BUTTERED SEA KALE

A native plant common to shingle beaches, sea kale (*Crambe maritime*) was traditionally used as a remedy against scurvy. Its beautiful blanched young leaves were considered a culinary delicacy until the eighteenth century when it fell out of favour. At J Sheekey it is still in vogue. Available from specialist suppliers from January to March.

SERVES 4

SEA KALE	100g
SALT	
SUNFLOWER OIL	For frying
RED MULLET FILLETS	4 x 200g
BUTTER SAUCE (*SEE BELOW*)	200ml
CHERVIL	Small bunch, chopped
FRESHLY GROUND BLACK PEPPER	

FOR THE BUTTER SAUCE
(yields approximately 200ml)

SUNFLOWER OIL	For frying
SHALLOTS	2, finely sliced
WHITE WINE VINEGAR	100ml
WHITE WINE	100ml
FISH STOCK	100ml
DOUBLE CREAM	30ml
UNSALTED BUTTER	200g, cold and diced
LEMON	½, juiced
SALT AND FRESHLY GROUND BLACK PEPPER	

To make the butter sauce, heat the oil in a heavy-bottomed saucepan and add the shallots. Cook for 2 minutes without colour. Add the white wine vinegar, bring to the boil and simmer until almost evaporated. Repeat this process with the wine. And again with the fish stock (see page 37, but a good quality cube is fine). Pour in the cream, bring to the boil and reduce by half. Whisk in the butter until you have a rich, glossy sauce. Sieve into a clean pan and season. Add lemon juice. Keep warm.

Cook the sea kale in boiling salted water for about 3 minutes, until tender. Drain in a colander, put into cold water and then drain again. Cut in half lengthways on the diagonal.

Heat the oil in a non-stick frying pan. Season the mullet fillets and cook skin-side down. This should take around 3 minutes. Turn the fish over and take off the heat, but keep in the pan (the heat of the pan will gently cook the other side).

In a small saucepan, re-heat the butter sauce and check seasoning, but do not boil or it will separate. Add the sea kale and the chervil.

Arrange the red mullet on a serving dish and finish with the butter sauce. At J Sheekey, we serve this with heritage potatoes, such as Pink Fir Apple.

SALT-BAKED SEA BASS

A delicious way to cook firm-textured fish such as bass, bream and snapper: sealing and cooking a whole fish without any juices or flavour escaping. At J Sheekey we have developed a ready-boned version so the fish can be quickly served. At home, try an unfilleted fish if you're confident about serving at the table. Otherwise, ask the fishmonger to bone the bass from the belly, leaving the head and tail on – a bit like a kipper – removing the backbone and the small pin bones that run down the fillets.

SERVES 4

COARSE SEA SALT	1kg
TABLE SALT	200g
SEA BASS	1.5kg, whole or boned as above
FENNEL	½ bulb, thinly sliced
DILL	½ bunch
FRESHLY GROUND BLACK PEPPER	
EXTRA VIRGIN OLIVE OIL OR MELTED UNSALTED BUTTER	To serve

An hour before cooking the fish, add a cupful of water to the salts and mix in a bowl to the consistency of a snowball.

Pre-heat the oven to 200°C / gas mark 6.

Spread a thin layer of the salt on a baking tray. Fill the fish's stomach with all of the fennel and most of the dill, and season with pepper. Lay the bass on the bed of salt and cover it with the rest, leaving the head free, creating a crust about 1cm thick, moulding it firmly with your hands. Bake the fish for 45 minutes.

The following you can do either at the table or in the kitchen, depending on how confident you feel (perhaps after showing your guests the dish as it comes out of the oven). Have warm plates ready and a large clean plate for the bits. Crack the salt a couple of times with the back of a heavy knife and carefully scrape it away from the fish, ensuring you remove as much as possible. Remove the head and tail and cut the fish through the body into even-sized portions, giving the underside a final check for salt before transferring it to the plates.

In a small saucepan, add either olive oil or a little butter (according to taste) and gently heat with the remaining dill, finely chopped. Serve drizzled over the fish, with simply cooked green vegetables or a salad.

WHOLE HERB-ROASTED SEA BREAM

Widely available all year round, British sea bream, often referred to in fishmongers as black bream (although they are more silver than black) is, along with pollack and mackerel, one of our most sustainable fish. Confusingly, 'sea bream' can also mean European red bream or Mediterranean gilt head, which are increasingly intensively farmed. Prized for its firm white flesh, bream can be filleted and grilled, fried, even barbecued. Sometimes, though, fish deserve to be cooked on the bone and served whole – this is one of those times.

SERVES 4

WHOLE SEA BREAM	4 x 400g, head on, scaled and gutted
SUNFLOWER OIL	For brushing
FLAT LEAF PARSLEY	½ bunch, stalks retained, leaves chopped
ROSEMARY	½ bunch, stalks retained, leaves chopped
THYME	½ bunch, stalks retained, leaves chopped
EXTRA VIRGIN OLIVE OIL	20ml
LEMON	1
SALT AND FRESHLY GROUND BLACK PEPPER	

Pre-heat the oven to 200°C / gas mark 6.

Rinse the fish, inside and out, and pat dry. Stuff its cavity with the stalks of the parsley, rosemary and thyme, half a sliced lemon, season and brush with sunflower oil.

Roast in the oven for approximately 12 minutes. The fish will feel firm to the touch when it's cooked.

In a small saucepan, warm through the olive oil with the chopped herbs, the juice of half a lemon and a pinch of salt and pepper.

Serve on plates and drizzle the fish with the warm olive oil, lemon and herb dressing.

Newlyn harbour, 6.20am, it is cold. Red-faced fishermen scurry to the market. Huge hook-beaked, black-backed gulls scream as they circle the dark sky overhead. A laden local boat sitting deep in the water unloads 30 tonnes of herring, purse-netted overnight in St Ives Bay. 'There are hundreds of tonnes out there,' the skipper grins as his shimmering fish are packed in ice. Herring, sardines and anchovies have returned to the teeming sea off the southern tip of Cornwall where Matthew Stevens buys prime fish for J Sheekey. We duck into the auction room where bidding is about to start on steely pollack, moss-coloured cod, ling, turbot, red mullet and gurnard, lemon and Dover sole, and squid and inky cuttlefish that have been landed overnight.

Stevens comes from a line of St Ives fishermen (his father, grandfather and great-grandfather were all called Matthew and all made their living from these waters). But today, Matthew Stevens' skill lies, not in buying at the market, though he is good at that, but in forging long relationships with the best fishermen and buying direct from their boat (he has been known to wait on the beach for hours for the right catch and craft to pull up on the sand).

Later, we will watch his filleters slice along the long spine and ribs of needle-toothed hake, with knife skills and an easy elegance that would shame a Japanese chef. We will admire the opalescent sheen of spanking fresh Cornish cod as it is packed to be dispatched to our kitchens the same day. We will eat butterflied sardines netted just off the coast a couple of hours earlier.

For now, though, the auction is over, there are sea stories to be shared, old friendships and rivalries to be nurtured. The market empties out, the herring catch is sold and everyone heads to The Sailors' Mission for mugs of tea and toast. It is not yet fully light and there are many boats to meet.

MONKFISH OSSO BUCCO WITH GREMOLATA

Classic osso bucco (veal shin 'bone with a hole') is a richly flavoured Milanese dish of braised meat and vegetables, traditionally served with gremolata. Monkfish adapts well to this technique.

SERVES 4

MONKFISH TAILS	2 x 250g, skinned and cut into steaks
PLAIN FLOUR	For dusting
SALT AND FRESHLY GROUND BLACK PEPPER	
EXTRA VIRGIN OLIVE OIL	For frying

FOR THE SAUCE

UNSALTED BUTTER	60g
ONION	1 small, peeled and finely chopped
GARLIC	1 clove, peeled and crushed
CARROT	1, peeled and finely chopped
CELERY	2 sticks, finely chopped
SAFFRON STRANDS	Pinch
THYME	3 sprigs, chopped
TOMATO PUREE	2 tbsp
WHITE WINE	125ml
BEEF STOCK	250ml

FOR THE GREMOLATA

GARLIC	2 cloves, peeled and crushed
LEMON	1, finely grated
FLAT LEAF PARSLEY	½ bunch, finely chopped
EXTRA VIRGIN OLIVE OIL	3 tbsp
SALT AND FRESHLY GROUND BLACK PEPPER	

First make the gremolata. Mix all the ingredients together and season. Set aside until required.

Pre-heat the oven to 200ºC / gas mark 6.

Make the sauce by melting half the butter in a heavy-bottomed saucepan and gently cooking the onion, garlic, carrot and celery until soft. Be careful not to let them colour. Keep the rest of the butter cold for finishing off the sauce. Add the saffron, thyme and tomato purée and cook for a minute or so. Stir in the white wine and reduce by three quarters. Add the beef stock (a good quality cube is fine). Bring to the boil and simmer until reduced by half. Set aside until the monkfish is ready.

Lightly flour, season and oil the monkfish. Heat a non-stick frying pan until it's smoking. Add the fish and cook for 3 minutes on each side until golden brown. Place in an oven-proof dish and transfer to the oven for around 8 minutes.

To serve, re-heat the sauce and whisk in the rest of the butter, diced. Place the monkfish on plates and spoon the sauce over the top. Drizzle with the gremolata.

MONKFISH AND PRAWN CURRY WITH BUTTERNUT SQUASH, ALMONDS AND BASMATI RICE

Firm-fleshed monkfish lends itself to Asian cooking styles. In our opinion, it is the ideal fish for curry. The number of ingredients for the sauce may appear a bit daunting at first, but don't worry, it is not difficult. Some dishes deserve a little more effort.

SERVES 6, GENEROUSLY

SUNFLOWER OIL	For frying
MONKFISH FILLETS	300g, cut into large pieces
TIGER PRAWNS	250g, raw
BUTTERNUT SQUASH	1 medium, peeled, cut into chunks and roasted (see page 232)
CORIANDER	½ small bunch, roughly chopped
GREEK YOGHURT	1 small tub
TOASTED FLAKED ALMONDS	3 tbsp

FOR THE RICE

BASMATI RICE	600g
CINNAMON STICK	½
CARDAMOM PODS	3, crushed
SALT	
UNSALTED BUTTER	50g

For the curry, heat the oil in a heavy-bottomed saucepan and add the cumin, fenugreek and mustard seeds. Cook on a medium heat until they start to crackle. Add cumin powder, turmeric, saffron, curry powder, cinnamon stick, bay leaf, paprika and cloves. Stir well. Cook out on a medium heat for 5 minutes. If it starts to stick, add a little cold water. Add onions, aubergine, garlic, ginger and chillis. Cook for around 10 minutes until soft, adding a little water from time to time. Stir in the tomato purée and stock (see page 70 for vegetable stock, but a good quality cube is fine), bring to the boil and cook for 20 minutes. Finally, add the lemon juice, coconut milk and ground almonds and cook for a further 10 minutes. Remove from the heat and allow to cool. Remove the cinnamon stick and bay leaf, and liquidise until smooth. Keep warm in a large pan.

Thoroughly wash the rice 3 or 4 times in cold water before cooking. Bring a saucepan of water to the boil, add the cinnamon stick and crushed cardamom pods to infuse. Add salt. Add the rice and simmer for 10 minutes until the rice is tender, but not mushy. Taste occasionally to check. Remove from the heat and drain well. Place the rice back into the pan, add the butter and cover with the lid until you're ready to serve.

SUNFLOWER OIL	2 tbsp
CUMIN SEEDS	1 tsp
FENUGREEK SEEDS	½ tsp
MUSTARD SEEDS	½ tsp
CUMIN POWDER	½ tsp
TURMERIC	1 tsp
SAFFRON STRANDS	Pinch
MILD CURRY POWDER	2 tbsp
CINNAMON STICK	½
BAY LEAF	1
PAPRIKA	½ tsp
WHOLE CLOVES	2
ONIONS	2 medium, finely sliced
AUBERGINE	1 medium, peeled and cut into chunks
GARLIC	3 cloves, peeled and crushed
FRESH GINGER	50g, peeled and grated
MILD CHILLIS	2, deseeded and finely chopped
TOMATO PUREE	2 tbsp
VEGETABLE OR CHICKEN STOCK	2 litres
LEMON	½, juiced
COCONUT MILK	1 x 160g tin
GROUND ALMONDS	40g
SALT AND FRESHLY GROUND BLACK PEPPER	

Heat a large non-stick frying pan until it's smoking, oil the monkfish and fry for about 3 minutes until golden brown. Add to the curry sauce, along with the roasted squash and prawns. Bring to the boil, simmer for 3 minutes, check seasoning and serve in a large bowl, topped with chopped coriander and flaked almonds. Serve with basmati rice and yoghurt on the side.

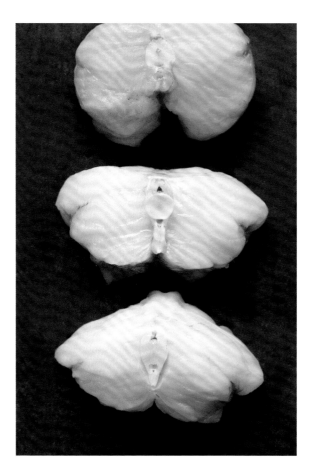

HAKE WITH BRAISED CANNELLINI BEANS AND SQUID

Hake's firm white flesh is much prized and sought after in Spain, where it is called *merluza*, and in Portugal, where it is known as *pescada*. Most hake caught in UK waters is exported, but a good fishmonger should carry it. With hake, it is particularly important to buy only the freshest fish.

SERVES 4

DRIED CANNELLINI BEANS	100g
EXTRA VIRGIN OLIVE OIL	60ml, plus a drizzle to finish
ONION	1, peeled and chopped into quarters
GARLIC	2 cloves, peeled and crushed
ROSEMARY	1 sprig, chopped
THYME	1 sprig, chopped
CHICKEN STOCK	500ml
SQUID	200g, cleaned and halved
SHALLOTS	2, peeled and finely diced
SMOKED PAPRIKA	1 tsp
CHERRY VINE TOMATOES	200g
TOMATO PUREE	2 tsp
WHITE WINE	125ml
UNSALTED BUTTER	60g
FLAT LEAF PARSLEY	½ small bunch, chopped
SALT AND FRESHLY GROUND BLACK PEPPER	
HAKE FILLETS	4 x 160g
LEMON	1

Firstly soak the cannellini beans in cold water overnight.

Pour 20ml olive oil into a heavy-bottomed saucepan. Gently cook the onion, 1 clove of garlic, rosemary and thyme for 5 minutes. Add the drained beans and chicken stock (a good quality cube is fine). Bring to the boil, season and simmer until the beans are soft but not mushy. You will notice that most of the stock will have evaporated. This should take around 30 minutes. Remove the onion, mindful that it will be very hot. Keep the cooked beans to one side.

Dice the squid. Heat a further 20ml olive oil in another saucepan and cook the shallots and squid for 2 to 3 minutes. Add paprika, the remaining garlic, cherry tomatoes, tomato purée and cook for a few minutes. Add the white wine, reduce by half, and add the beans. Keep on a low heat. Just before you're ready to serve, stir in the butter and parsley and adjust the seasoning.

Finally, heat a non-stick frying pan. Add the remaining olive oil. Season the hake fillets and gently cook skin-side down for 5 minutes. Turn over for a further 4 minutes.

To serve, place a spoonful of the cooked beans onto each plate. Place the hake on top and drizzle with olive oil and a squeeze of lemon.

CORNISH FISH STEW

Our British take on bouillabaisse, the provençal fish stew from Marseilles. We choose from a combination of cod, turbot, John Dory, halibut and monkfish to go with the all-important gurnard, but if your choice or budget is limited, just use the firmest and freshest you can find.

SERVES 4–6

EXTRA VIRGIN OLIVE OIL	2 tbsp
ASSORTED WHITE FISH FILLETS	400g
GURNARD FILLETS	2 x 100g, cut in half
SCALLOPS	4, shelled
CORNISH FISH SOUP (*SEE PAGE 92*)	400ml
FENNEL	1 bulb, finely sliced
TOMATOES	100g, diced
MUSSELS	200g, cleaned
WHITE CRAB MEAT	50g
HERBS (*EG CHERVIL, FLAT LEAF PARSLEY, DILL AND TARRAGON*)	½ bunch, chopped
SAFFRON MAYONNAISE (*SEE PAGE 93*)	To serve

Pour half the olive oil into a non-stick frying pan and fry the white fish and gurnard for 2 minutes on each side. Set aside.

Wipe the pan with kitchen roll and add the remaining olive oil. Sauté the scallops for 1 minute on each side. Remove and keep to one side.

Re-heat the fish soup in a large oven-proof casserole. Bring to the boil, add finely sliced fennel, tomatoes and mussels. When the mussels have opened, add the fish, scallops, crab meat and chopped herbs. Cook for a further 2 to 3 minutes and serve directly from the casserole with crusty bread and saffron mayonnaise.

Mixed herbs add an aromatic note to the stew, although as a base for moules marinières, for a vongole, in a court bouillon or for a simple white sauce with white fish, parsley is still the herb most often used here when cooking shellfish or fish. At J Sheekey, we also like cooking with chervil and tarragon for their aniseed tones.

DEVILLED WHOLE MACKEREL WITH TOMATO AND SHAVED FENNEL SALAD

According to Alan Davidson's *Oxford Companion to Food*, devilled as a culinary term 'first appeared as a noun in the eighteenth century, and then in the early nineteenth century as a verb meaning to cook something with fiery hot spices or condiments'. It works well here with the robust flavour and texture of mackerel.

SERVES 4

WHOLE MACKEREL	4 x 400–600g, gutted and cleaned
RIPE TOMATOES	500g mixed (different colours and sizes work well)
FENNEL	1 bulb
CHERVIL	Small bunch, chopped

FOR THE DRESSING

WHITE WINE VINEGAR	2 tbsp
EXTRA VIRGIN COLD PRESSED RAPESEED OIL	6 tbsp
EXTRA VIRGIN OLIVE OIL	4 tbsp
CASTER SUGAR	½ tsp
SALT AND FRESHLY GROUND BLACK PEPPER	

FOR THE DEVILLED PASTE

UNSALTED BUTTER	40g
CASTER SUGAR	1 tsp
ENGLISH MUSTARD POWDER	1 tsp
CAYENNE	1 tsp
PAPRIKA	1 tsp
GROUND CORIANDER	1 tsp
RED WINE VINEGAR	2 tbsp
FRESHLY GROUND BLACK PEPPER	1 tbsp
SALT	2 tsp

Firstly make the dressing. Put all the ingredients into a jar and shake until emulsified.

For the devilled paste, melt the butter in a heavy-bottomed saucepan, add the other ingredients and gently cook for 10 minutes, ensuring it doesn't burn. If necessary, add a tablespoon or two of water. The paste can be made a couple of days in advance, refrigerated and then brought back to room temperature before using.

Pre-heat the oven to 180°C / gas mark 4.

Score the mackerel at 2cm intervals along both sides. Rub the devilled paste over each fish and leave to marinate for 20 minutes. Bake in the oven for 10 to 12 minutes (depending on size), until the fish is firm and cooked throughout.

Slice the tomatoes (halving any small ones). Finely shave the fennel and place together with the tomatoes and chopped chervil in a bowl. Add most of the dressing and season.

To serve, cover a large serving plate with the tomato and fennel salad. Place the mackerel on top and drizzle over any excess dressing.

SALADS &
VEGETABLES

BEETROOT WITH RUBY LEAF AND POMEGRANATE

A strikingly beautiful salad, with the sweetness of the beetroot marrying well with the pomegranate.

SERVES 4

RED ENDIVE	2 heads
MIXED SALAD LEAVES, RUBY IF POSSIBLE	100g
BEETROOT	300g, cooked and roughly chopped
CHIVES	½ small bunch, chopped

FOR THE DRESSING

POMEGRANATE	1
WHITE WINE VINEGAR	1 tbsp
EXTRA VIRGIN OLIVE OIL	3 tbsp
EXTRA VIRGIN COLD PRESSED RAPESEED OIL	2 tbsp
CASTER SUGAR	Pinch
SALT AND FRESHLY GROUND BLACK PEPPER	

For the dressing, cut the pomegranate in two. Retain the seeds from one half, juice the other (see box). Pour the juice into a saucepan, bring to the boil and reduce by half. Excluding the seeds, mix the rest of the ingredients together in a bowl and season.

Trim the cores from the endives and separate the leaves, removing any that are discoloured. Mix with the ruby salad leaves, rinse together and dry. Transfer to a large bowl. Add the beetroot. Toss with the dressing and sprinkle the pomegranate seeds and chopped chives over the top. Season and serve.

HOW TO DESEED A POMEGRANATE
First cut off the 'crown end' and discard. Slice the rind in several places. Soak upside down in cold water for up to ten minutes. Keeping it in the bowl, break off the rind and remove the seeds from the membrane. The seeds will sink to the bottom. Skim off the rind and membrane with a slotted spoon. Drain the seeds in a colander. Pat dry. Will keep refrigerated in an airtight container for up to two days.

CHOPPED SALAD

A crisp, crunchy salad which can be the base for a main course, by adding prawns, bacon or smoked fish.

SERVES 4

RIPE TOMATOES	4
CELERY	2 stalks, peeled, leaves chopped
RIPE AVOCADO	1
CUCUMBER	½
RADISHES	½ bunch
WHITE ENDIVE	1 head, chopped
ROMAINE LETTUCE	2 heads, chopped
FLAT LEAF PARSLEY	1 small bunch, chopped
CHIVES	1 bunch, chopped
SALT AND FRESHLY GROUND BLACK PEPPER	

FOR THE DRESSING

DIJON MUSTARD	1 tbsp
WHITE WINE VINEGAR	1 tbsp
EXTRA VIRGIN OLIVE OIL	3 tbsp
EXTRA VIRGIN COLD PRESSED RAPESEED OIL	2 tbsp
LEMON	½, juiced
SALT AND FRESHLY GROUND BLACK PEPPER	

For the dressing, put all the ingredients into a jar and shake until emulsified.

Seed and dice the tomatoes. Cut the celery in half lengthways, then into 1cm pieces. Peel and dice the avocado into 1cm cubes. Dice the cucumber into 1cm cubes. Slice the radishes. Place all the salad ingredients in a large bowl, toss with the dressing and herbs. Season.

GREEN HERB SALAD

The leaves here are just a guide: use whatever salads are fresh, available and in season. Here the fennel and chervil add a hint of aniseed.

SERVES 4

WHITE ENDIVE	2 heads
FENNEL	1 bulb
GEM HEARTS	2 heads
WATERCRESS	Handful
CHIVES	Small bunch, chopped
CHERVIL	Small bunch, chopped
TARRAGON	5 sprigs, chopped
SALT AND FRESHLY GROUND BLACK PEPPER	

FOR THE DRESSING

DIJON MUSTARD	1 tsp
WHITE WINE VINEGAR	1 tbsp
EXTRA VIRGIN OLIVE OIL	3 tbsp
SUNFLOWER OIL	2 tbsp
CLEAR HONEY	1 tsp
LEMON	½, juiced
SALT AND FRESHLY GROUND BLACK PEPPER	

For the dressing, put all the ingredients into a jar and shake until emulsified.

For the salad, core the endives and separate the leaves. Finely slice the fennel. Place all the salad leaves into a large bowl and toss with the dressing. Finish with the chopped herbs and season.

ENDIVE, PEAR, STILTON AND WALNUT SALAD

An elegant English version of the French classic salad using Roquefort. Any fine blue cheese will work well for this recipe but we prefer to use Stilton.

SERVES 4

WALNUTS	30g
EXTRA VIRGIN OLIVE OIL	1 tbsp
SALT AND FRESHLY GROUND BLACK PEPPER	
WHITE ENDIVE	2 heads
RED ENDIVE	2 heads
RIPE PEAR	1, peeled, cored and sliced
STILTON	100g, broken into small pieces
CHIVES	½ small bunch, chopped

FOR THE DRESSING

STILTON	20g
DIJON MUSTARD	1 tsp
WHITE WINE VINEGAR	1 tbsp
EXTRA VIRGIN OLIVE OIL	3 tbsp
SUNFLOWER OIL	2 tbsp
CASTER SUGAR	Pinch

Pre-heat the grill. Toss the walnuts in olive oil and salt, place on a tray and grill until lightly toasted, about 3 minutes. Ensure they don't burn. Leave to cool.

To make the dressing, blend all the ingredients in a liquidiser until smooth. If it's too thick, thin down with a little water.

Core the endives and separate the leaves, placing them in a bowl, removing any that are discoloured.

To serve, arrange the endive leaves on a large serving plate with the slices of pear. Spoon the dressing over. Scatter the pieces of Stilton on top with the walnuts, chopped chives and freshly ground pepper.

CELERIAC REMOULADE

A classic winter salad common in France, where it is widely available in brasseries and corner shops, celeriac rémoulade is a good match for smoked fish and cold meats.

SERVES 4

DIJON MUSTARD	2 tbsp (more if you prefer stronger)
CORNICHONS	30g, finely chopped
CAPERS	20g
FLAT LEAF PARSLEY	¼ bunch, chopped
CHERVIL	¼ bunch, chopped
CHIVES	¼ bunch, chopped
MAYONNAISE (*SEE PAGE 56*)	200ml
CELERIAC	1 small, peeled
SALT AND FRESHLY GROUND BLACK PEPPER	

Place the mustard, cornichons, capers and chopped herbs into a large bowl and mix well with the mayonnaise.

Finely julienne the celeriac to matchstick size or shred with a mandolin. Add to the bowl and mix well. Season with salt and pepper and serve with grilled fish.

LETTUCE AND LOVAGE: WHAT WORKS WITH FISH

As with all things fish, the choice of garnish and side dish depends on the season and the style of fish you are serving. The key is not to overpower the fish but to match its intensity, texture and tone.

In summer, light and fresh combinations of, say, sorrel, peas and beans are a perfect accompaniment to new-season sea trout or salmon; fried courgette flowers or crushed broad beans are good with crab and British green asparagus is a great accompaniment to brown shrimp.

Unsurprisingly, many 'wild' or foraged foods work with wild fish, particularly if they are found on or near the shoreline. At J Sheekey, we serve sea purslane, parsley and cockles with a classic cod, while wilted sea beet and wild garlic will complement almost any white fish fillet. Summery marsh samphire is good in a red gurnard salad but will also add a briny crunch to crisp cod cheeks with tartare sauce. Further inland, wild mushrooms such as St George's mushrooms or girolles bring depth and sweet woody notes to brill, while ceps will add a richer, meatier, earthier tone to cooks' favourite cod tongues.

The southern Mediterranean countries also know a thing or two about fish dishes. Firm-fleshed hake favours braised cannellini beans, while roasted John Dory works with roasted tomatoes. A more robust oilier fish can take a sharper flavour. Lightly pickled fennel is a perfect partner for 'devilled' mackerel, and a spicy Moroccan-style salad is good with grilled sardines. In winter, though, try earthier northern flavours with fish, such as sweet beetroot with smoked mackerel, Irish colcannon with smoked haddock or a deep, caramelised cauliflower mash.

Above all, keep the combinations simple. All the dishes in the book come with serving suggestions and combinations from our many years of experience, but if in doubt you will not go too far wrong with a grilled fish, a green herb salad and buttery steamed potatoes.

SPROUTS AND TOPS WITH CRISPY BACON AND ROASTED CHESTNUTS

Under-appreciated, sprout tops are at their best at the start of the season around the beginning of October, when they are still sweet and tender.

SERVES 4

CHESTNUTS	100g fresh
BRUSSELS SPROUTS	500g small, outer leaves removed
SPROUT TOPS	250g, outer leaves removed, chopped
UNSALTED BUTTER	30g
STREAKY BACON	25g, cut into strips
SALT AND FRESHLY GROUND BLACK PEPPER	

Pre-heat the oven to 200°C / gas mark 6.

Using a sharp knife, cut a cross in the top of each chestnut. Place on a tray and roast for around 30 minutes until the skins split and the flesh is tender. Remove and peel while still warm.

Bring a large saucepan of salted water to the boil. Add the sprouts and cook for 10 minutes, or until tender. Remove with a slotted spoon and set aside. Bring the water back to the boil and cook the sprout tops until tender; this will take about 4 minutes. Drain thoroughly.

In another pan, heat the butter, add the bacon and cook till golden brown. Add the chestnuts, the drained sprouts and sprout tops. Toss together and cook for 2 or 3 minutes. Check seasoning and serve.

CREAMED SWEETCORN, CHILLI AND BASIL

Delicious in late summer when sweetcorn is widely available. Here, we have added a little spice and basil.

SERVES 4

UNSALTED BUTTER	25g
SHALLOTS	2, sliced
MILD CHILLI	1 medium, deseeded and chopped
SWEETCORN KERNELS	500g
VEGETABLE STOCK	50ml
DOUBLE CREAM	100ml
BASIL	¼ small bunch
SALT AND FRESHLY GROUND BLACK PEPPER	

In a saucepan, melt the butter and add shallots and chilli. Cook until soft, but not coloured. Add sweetcorn. Cook for a minute, stirring it into the shallot and chilli mixture. Add vegetable stock (see page 70, but a good quality cube is fine), bring to the boil and simmer for 5 minutes until the stock has almost evaporated. Add the cream, bring to the boil and reduce by half. Coarsely blitz in a liquidiser.

Return to a saucepan to heat gently through. Scatter with torn basil leaves, season and serve.

SAUTEED WILD MUSHROOMS WITH ROASTED GARLIC

Mushroom hunting is now fashionable but, if foraging, please use a reputable guide or book and be very careful; if in any doubt, do not eat! Otherwise, stick to a trusted supplier, specialist store or supermarket. Ceps, girolles, chanterelles, horn of plenty or pieds de mouton will all work well.

SERVES 4

WILD MUSHROOMS	500g, cleaned
EXTRA VIRGIN OLIVE OIL	30ml
SHALLOT	1 large, finely chopped
UNSALTED BUTTER	40g
FLAT LEAF PARSLEY	¼ small bunch, chopped
SALT AND FRESHLY GROUND BLACK PEPPER	

FOR THE ROASTED GARLIC

GARLIC	1 bulb
EXTRA VIRGIN OLIVE OIL	
SALT AND FRESHLY GROUND BLACK PEPPER	

Pre-heat the oven to 190°C / gas mark 5.

Season the garlic bulb with olive oil, salt and pepper. Cover with foil and roast in the oven for 30 minutes, or until soft.

Clean and prepare the mushrooms (avoid getting them wet), keeping them whole or as chunky as possible. Heat the oil in a heavy-bottomed saucepan and gently cook the shallots with 4 cloves of the roasted garlic (removed from their skin) for 2 to 3 minutes until the shallots are soft.

Add the mushrooms, season and sauté for 4 to 5 minutes. When the mushrooms are soft, add the butter. Cook for a further minute, add the chopped parsley and serve.

If you are using different varieties of wild mushroom, the softer or smaller ones will need to be added later in the cooking process.

SPRING PEAS WITH LETTUCE AND LOVAGE

Lovage is from the same *umbelliferae* family as carrot, parsley, fennel and angelica. Used sparingly, its seeds, leaves and stem work well in soups and salads, especially with tomatoes.

SERVES 4

PEAS	200g, shelled or frozen
UNSALTED BUTTER	30g
LITTLE GEMS	2 heads, shredded
LOVAGE LEAVES	5
PEA SHOOTS	Handful
SALT AND FRESHLY GROUND BLACK PEPPER	

Bring a saucepan of water to the boil, add the peas and cook till tender. Drain and keep to one side.

Meanwhile, heat the butter in a saucepan, add the lettuce, lovage and pea shoots. Gently cook until wilted. Add the peas, season and serve.

SPROUTING BROCCOLI WITH CHILLI AND LEMON ZEST

If you can't find purple sprouting broccoli, use tender-stem broccoli or, if you can find it, *cime di rapa*, a brassica related to turnip and sometimes known as *broccoletti*, rapini or broccoli raab.

SERVES 4

PURPLE SPROUTING BROCCOLI	400g
EXTRA VIRGIN OLIVE OIL	For frying
MILD CHILLI	1 medium, deseeded and finely sliced
LEMON	1, finely grated
SALT AND FRESHLY GROUND BLACK PEPPER	

Place the broccoli into a saucepan of boiling salted water and cook for 3 to 4 minutes. Do not overcook. Drain.

Heat the olive oil in a frying pan, add the chilli and cook for a minute or two. Add the broccoli and lemon zest, tossing together to ensure the broccoli is well coated. Remove from the heat. Season and serve.

SPRING VEGETABLES WITH TARRAGON BUTTER

A celebration of spring and the arrival of fresh new green ingredients.

SERVES 4

BROAD BEANS	100g, podded
PEAS	100g, shelled or frozen
GREEN ASPARAGUS	250g medium, half-peeled, woody stems removed
RADISHES	½ bunch
UNSALTED BUTTER	20g
TARRAGON	4 sprigs, leaves removed and chopped
PEA SHOOTS OR WATERCRESS	1 bunch
SALT AND FRESHLY GROUND BLACK PEPPER	

To keep the vegetables green and full of flavour, boil separately in a saucepan of salted water until just soft. If the broad beans are large, pop the skins off with your fingers. If not, they'll be fine unpeeled. Plunge into a bowl of iced water and drain.

Blanch the radishes for 1 minute and then plunge into cold water and drain.

Melt the butter in a heavy-bottomed saucepan and add the tarragon. Add the cooked vegetables and radishes, warm through and finish with pea shoots, allowing them to wilt down slightly. Season and serve.

BUTTERED GREENS WITH HAZELNUTS

Instead of hazelnuts, you can use Kentish cobnuts in season – mid August to October – or walnuts.

SERVES 4

HAZELNUTS	20g (shelled weight)
MIX OF SPRING GREENS, SAVOY OR HISPI (POINTED) CABBAGE, SPROUT TOPS	1kg, trimmed and stalks removed
UNSALTED BUTTER	65g
SALT AND FRESHLY GROUND BLACK PEPPER	

Pre-heat the grill to a medium temperature, roughly chop the nuts and lightly toast on a baking tray. Watch them carefully so they don't burn. Season with salt.

Chop the greens and cook in plenty of boiling salted water for 4 to 5 minutes until tender. Drain thoroughly.

Melt the butter in a saucepan and add the toasted nuts. Add the greens, toss together, season and serve.

Hazel is still used for hedging, coppicing and for bean sticks as well as for nut growing in the UK. Now concentrate here: hazelnuts are also called cobnuts although 'Kentish cobnuts' are actually filberts from the same *Corylus* species. Kentish cobnuts are mostly sold young in autumn and retain a greener, fresher texture and flavour; they are best eaten quickly from the shell. Hazelnuts are dried to last the winter months and, as with all nuts, should not be stored in tins.

PARMESAN-FRIED COURGETTES AND FLOWERS WITH TOMATO RELISH

Courgette flowers can be found at good farmers' markets, 'pick your own' farms, specialist stores and even some supermarkets. Traditionally eaten in southern Europe on Easter fasting days, they are mostly available from summer to early autumn. If flowers are not to be found, add more courgettes.

SERVES 4

SUNFLOWER OIL	For frying
COURGETTE FLOWERS	2, cut in half lengthways
COURGETTES	3 large, sliced diagonally
PLAIN FLOUR	For dusting
FREE RANGE EGG	1 medium, beaten
FRESH WHITE BREADCRUMBS	100g
FRESHLY GRATED PARMESAN	30g
SALT AND FRESHLY GROUND BLACK PEPPER	

FOR THE TOMATO RELISH

EXTRA VIRGIN OLIVE OIL	40ml
ONION	1 medium, peeled and finely chopped
MILD CHILLI	½ medium, deseeded and finely chopped
GARLIC	2 cloves, peeled and crushed
THYME	2 sprigs, chopped
ROSEMARY	2 sprigs, chopped
OREGANO	2 sprigs, chopped
BALSAMIC VINEGAR	2 tbsp
TOMATO PUREE	1 tbsp
CHOPPED TOMATOES	1 x 400g tin
SALT AND FRESHLY GROUND BLACK PEPPER	
FLAT LEAF PARSLEY	½ small bunch, chopped

Firstly make the tomato relish. Heat the oil in a heavy-bottomed saucepan and gently cook the onions, chilli, garlic and herbs (except parsley) for about 5 minutes without allowing them to colour.

Add the balsamic vinegar and reduce by half. Add the purée, cook for a minute, then add the chopped tomatoes. Bring to the boil and simmer for 20 minutes. The consistency should be like chutney. If it is too runny, continue to simmer. Season and leave to cool. When cool, add the parsley.

For the courgettes, pour 6cm of oil into a medium-sized heavy-bottomed saucepan, or use a deep fat fryer. Heat to 160°C. If using a saucepan, please be careful as the oil will be very hot. Dip the courgettes and flowers in the flour, then egg, then breadcrumbs. Fry until golden brown. Remove with tongs and place onto kitchen paper to soak up excess oil. Season.

Arrange the courgettes and flowers on a large serving dish. Dust with grated Parmesan and serve with the tomato relish on the side.

CAULIFLOWER GRATIN

A perfect cheese sauce without the time and effort of making a béchamel.

SERVES 4

CAULIFLOWER	1 large
UNSALTED BUTTER	50g
GRATED CHEDDAR CHEESE	100g

FOR THE CHEESE SAUCE

DOUBLE CREAM	250ml
MASCARPONE	500g
FRESHLY GRATED PARMESAN	120g
SALT AND GROUND WHITE PEPPER	

Remove any green stalk from the cauliflower and roughly chop into small florets. Rinse and drain.

For the sauce, bring the double cream and mascarpone to the boil in a heavy-bottomed saucepan. Add the Parmesan and simmer for 5 minutes. Season. Liquidise until smooth and then strain through a sieve.

Steam the cauliflower florets for 5 minutes, or until tender. Gently melt the butter in a pan, add the cauliflower, then the sauce, ensuring you cover all the cauliflower. Place in a heat-proof dish, top with the grated Cheddar and glaze under the grill or in the oven until golden brown. Serve immediately.

ROASTED SQUASH WITH PUMPKIN SEED PESTO

A richly flavoured autumn dish for when delicious varieties of pumpkin and squash come into season.

SERVES 4–6

MIXED SQUASH	1.5kg, peeled, deseeded and chopped into 4cm pieces
EXTRA VIRGIN OLIVE OIL	For roasting
SALT AND FRESHLY GROUND BLACK PEPPER	
	FOR THE PUMPKIN SEED PESTO
PUMPKIN SEEDS	100g
FRESHLY GRATED PARMESAN	50g
FLAT LEAF PARSLEY	½ small bunch, chopped
EXTRA VIRGIN OLIVE OIL	60ml
SALT AND FRESHLY GROUND BLACK PEPPER	

Pre-heat the oven to 190ºC / gas mark 5.

Heat a roasting tray in the oven. Toss the squash with the olive oil in a bowl and season. Place on the hot tray and cook for 30 minutes, or until nicely coloured and cooked through.

For the pumpkin seed pesto, lightly toast the pumpkin seeds on a very low heat. You don't need oil for this, but keep your eye on the pan, as the seeds can easily burn. Put the seeds, Parmesan, parsley and olive oil into a food processor and blitz. Add more oil if needed: the consistency should be slightly runny. Season to taste.

To serve, arrange the squash on a serving dish and toss over the pumpkin seed pesto.

SAMPHIRE AND VEGETABLE FRITTERS

Tempura flour makes the dish light and crisp and is an interesting alternative to simply steamed samphire.

SERVES 4

SAMPHIRE	100g
SPRING ONIONS	½ bunch, trimmed and chopped on the angle
CARROT	1, peeled and sliced into thin strips
MANGETOUT	100g, sliced into thin strips
COURGETTE	1, sliced into thin strips
CORIANDER	½ small bunch, finely chopped
SESAME SEEDS	2 tsp
ICED WATER	
TEMPURA FLOUR	150g
SUNFLOWER OIL	For frying
SALT AND GROUND WHITE PEPPER	

In a large bowl, mix all of the vegetables with the coriander and sesame seeds.

For the batter, in another large bowl, slowly add iced water to the tempura flour. Whisk continuously, until you get a consistency of pouring cream. Stir the vegetables into the batter and season.

Pour 6cm of oil into a large heavy-bottomed saucepan or a deep fat fryer. Heat to 160°C. If using a saucepan, please be careful as the oil will be very hot. Fry the vegetables in small batches until golden brown. Remove with tongs and place onto kitchen paper to soak up any excess oil. Season if necessary. You can serve with chilli jam (see page 26).

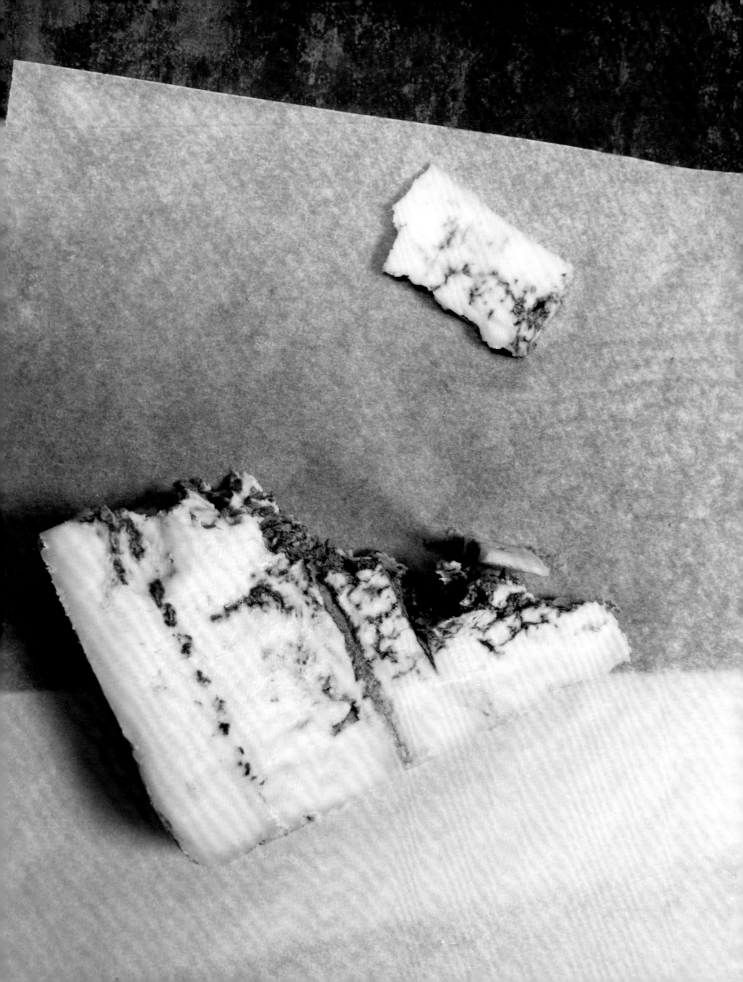

SAVOURIES

WELSH RAREBIT

The essential British savoury and the one that everyone eats at home with or without Worcestershire sauce (which we recommend). No-one really knows any more how cheese on toast came to be called 'rabbit' or 'rarebit'. What we do know is that both Escoffier and Brillat-Savarin gave a recipe for lapin gallois and a wouelsche rabette first appeared in Antoine Beauvilliers' *L'Art du Cuisinier* in 1814. Our trusted recipe is not quite as old, though we believe it is definitive.

SERVES 4

GUINNESS	80ml
DOUBLE CREAM	80ml
GRATED CHEDDAR CHEESE	150g
ENGLISH MUSTARD	1 tsp
WORCESTERSHIRE SAUCE	2 tsp
FREE RANGE EGG YOLKS	2 medium
SALT AND FRESHLY GROUND BLACK PEPPER	
BLOOMER-STYLE BREAD	4 slices

Simmer Guinness in a saucepan until it has reduced by half. Add cream and reduce by half again. Remove and leave to cool. Stir in cheese, mustard, Worcestershire sauce and egg yolks. Season.

Pre-heat the grill. Toast the bread on both sides, spread the cheese mixture on top (about 1cm thick), right to the edges to avoid burning. Grill on a medium heat until nicely browned.

Serve with a bottle of Worcestershire sauce on the side.

At J Sheekey Oyster Bar, we serve smoked haddock rarebit using this recipe, but folding pieces of poached smoked haddock into the cheese mixture. Also a perfect supper 'bucked' with a poached egg on top.

HERRING ROES ON TOAST WITH CAPERS

Soft herring roes were once a staple of many a child's tea and still sell well at J Sheekey. Also known as milts, they are more normally sold frozen, though they can be found fresh during spring and early summer. Frozen roes are fine here.

SERVES 4

SOFT HERRING ROES	400–450g
MILK	To cover
BAY LEAF	1
THYME	3 sprigs
SUNFLOWER OIL	For frying
PLAIN FLOUR	For dusting
UNSALTED BUTTER	100g
TOAST (*A BLOOMER-STYLE LOAF IS GOOD*)	4 thick slices
CAPERS	60g
FLAT LEAF PARSLEY	½ bunch, finely chopped
LEMON	1, juiced
SALT AND GROUND WHITE PEPPER	

Put the herring roes in a saucepan and cover with milk, bay leaf, thyme and a pinch of salt. Bring to the boil and simmer for 2 minutes. Remove roes and drain on kitchen paper.

Heat the oil in a non-stick frying pan. Lightly flour the roes and fry until golden brown. Add half the butter and continue cooking for another 2 minutes. Remove and arrange on toast.

Put the rest of the butter into the frying pan and heat until foaming (being careful not to burn). Add capers, parsley and lemon juice, stir well, season and spoon over the roes.

SMOKED COD ROE ON TOAST WITH HORSERADISH BUTTER

Under-appreciated here, though revered in other countries, you may need to order smoked cod roe from your fishmonger.

SERVES 4

WATERCRESS	100g
EXTRA VIRGIN OLIVE OIL	2 tbsp
LEMON	½, juiced
FRESH HORSERADISH ROOT	2cm, grated
SALT AND FRESHLY GROUND BLACK PEPPER	
STONE BAKED OR SOURDOUGH BREAD	4 slices
SMOKED COD ROE	1 x 200g, thinly sliced

FOR THE HORSERADISH BUTTER

UNSALTED BUTTER	100g, softened
CREAMED HORSERADISH	2 tbsp
CHIVES	½ bunch, chopped

For the horseradish butter, ensure the butter is at room temperature. Mix creamed horseradish, butter and chives in a bowl. This will keep for up to a week in the fridge, covered with Clingfilm.

Toss the watercress with olive oil, lemon juice and grated horseradish in a bowl. Season.

Toast the bread, spread with the horseradish butter and top with thin slices of smoked cod roe. Grill for 2 minutes. Place onto individual plates and serve with the watercress salad.

CRISP FRIED ST EADBURGHA WITH GOOSEBERRY CHUTNEY

A hand-made organic cheese from the edge of the Vale of Evesham, St Eadburgha is named after the saint of the Saxon church in the local town of Broadway, but any Camembert-style cheese will work well here.

SERVES 4

SUNFLOWER OIL	For frying
ST EADBURGHA	250g
PLAIN FLOUR	For dusting
FREE RANGE EGG	1 medium, beaten
FRESH WHITE BREADCRUMBS	100g
SALT AND FRESHLY GROUND BLACK PEPPER	
CELERY	4 sticks, peeled and trimmed

FOR THE GOOSEBERRY CHUTNEY

GOOSEBERRIES	500g
ONION	120g, finely chopped
WATER	125ml
CASTER SUGAR	225g
MUSTARD SEEDS	1 tsp
CINNAMON STICK	½
GROUND GINGER	½ tbsp
CAYENNE	¼ tbsp
DISTILLED VINEGAR	250ml
SALT	1 tsp

Firstly prepare the chutney. Top and tail the gooseberries and wash thoroughly. Place in a heavy-bottomed saucepan with the finely chopped onion and water. Bring to the boil and when the gooseberries start to soften, add the remaining ingredients and simmer for 1 hour until the mixture starts to become thick and syrupy. Remove from the heat and leave to cool. Pour the chutney into an airtight container and store in the refrigerator until ready for use. If sealed properly and kept refrigerated it can last for up to a month.

Cut the cheese into 8 wedges. Dip the wedges in the flour, then egg, then breadcrumbs.

Pour 6cm of oil into a medium-sized heavy-bottomed saucepan, or use a deep fat fryer. Heat to 140°C. If using a saucepan, please be careful as the oil will be very hot.

Fry until golden brown. Remove with tongs and place onto kitchen paper to soak up excess oil. Season.

Place 2 wedges of the cheese and a spoonful of gooseberry chutney onto each plate. Serve with the celery sticks (for dipping).

TAPENADE

The ubiquitous provençal hors d'oeuvre, whose name comes from *tapenas*, provençal for capers.

SERVES 4

KALAMATA OLIVES	250g, pitted
CAPERS	20g
ANCHOVY FILLETS	6, chopped
GARLIC	1 clove, peeled and crushed
LEMON	½, juiced
EXTRA VIRGIN OLIVE OIL	2–4 tbsp

Place olives, capers, anchovy fillets, garlic and lemon juice into a food processor and mix, while slowly adding as much olive oil as necessary to form a paste. Check seasoning.

EGGS ARLINGTON

Perfect brunch: classic poached egg, smoked salmon, hollandaise sauce, named in honour of our sister restaurant Le Caprice in Arlington Street, London St James's.

SERVES 4

ENGLISH MUFFINS	2, halved
FREE RANGE EGGS	4 medium
SMOKED SALMON	4 slices
HOLLANDAISE SAUCE (*SEE PAGE 116*)	120ml
SALT AND GROUND WHITE PEPPER	

Lightly toast the muffins and poach the eggs (see page 94).

Place a slice of smoked salmon on the muffin with poached egg on top and coat with generous spoonfuls of hollandaise. Season.

SMOKED SALMON AND PARMESAN STRAWS

A popular savoury nibble. For more information on smoked salmon supplier Brown and Forrest, see page 88.

MAKES 15–20 STRAWS

PUFF PASTRY	200g
PLAIN FLOUR	For dusting
FREE RANGE EGG YOLK	1 medium
SMOKED SALMON	100g
FRESHLY GRATED PARMESAN	2 tbsp
FRESHLY GROUND BLACK PEPPER	

Pre-heat the oven to 180°C / gas mark 4.

On a floured surface, roll out the puff pastry sheet to a thickness of around 4mm. Brush the pastry with egg yolk and lay smoked salmon on top. Sprinkle liberally with the Parmesan and season with black pepper. Cut into strips 2cm wide.

Lay the pastry strips on a greased baking tray at least 2cm apart (as they will expand and move during cooking). Hold each pastry strip at both ends and twist in opposite directions. Sprinkle with a little more Parmesan.

Bake for 10 to 12 minutes, or until golden.

BLACK FIGS WITH MELTED GORGONZOLA

Ripe figs with ripe cheese, a soft and luscious Mediterranean-inspired dish.

SERVES 4

BLACK FIGS	8, ripe
GORGONZOLA	160g
EXTRA VIRGIN OLIVE OIL	3 tbsp
BALSAMIC VINEGAR	1 tbsp
ROCKET	100g
SALT AND FRESHLY GROUND BLACK PEPPER	
FOCACCIA OR CIABATTA BREAD	

Pre-heat the oven to 200°C / gas mark 6.

Place the figs in an oven-proof dish. Make a cross in the top of the figs and pinch the bottoms so they fan out. Insert pieces of Gorgonzola in each fig.

Drizzle the figs with a little olive oil and season. Bake for about 8 minutes until the cheese has melted.

Serve the figs on a slate or a large serving dish with rocket tossed in balsamic and the remaining oil and grilled focaccia or ciabatta.

BAKED VACHERIN WITH ENDIVE SALAD AND TOASTED BAGUETTE

One of our favourite winter cheeses, Vacherin (or Mont d'Or, as it is also known) comes in its own spruce box, allowing it to liquefy as it ripens. We sometimes eat it as it is, with a spoon. But baked in the box is when it comes into its own as a simple fondue without the clearing up. This is not really a recipe, more a temperature suggestion, but the combination with the bitterness of the chicory works beautifully.

SERVES 4

VACHERIN	1, approximately 400g
FOR THE ENDIVE SALAD	
WHITE ENDIVE	2 heads
RED ENDIVE	1 head
DIJON MUSTARD	1 tbsp
WHITE WINE VINEGAR	1 tbsp
EXTRA VIRGIN OLIVE OIL	2 tbsp
SUNFLOWER OIL	2 tbsp
SALT AND FRESHLY GROUND BLACK PEPPER	
BAGUETTE	1, sliced and lightly toasted

To make the salad, core the endives and separate the leaves, removing any that are discoloured. In a salad bowl, whisk together the mustard and white wine vinegar. Gradually whisk in the oils and season. Toss the leaves in the dressing.

Pre-heat the oven to 180°C / gas mark 5.

Wrap and seal the boxed Vacherin in foil and bake in the oven for 15 to 20 minutes. Remove the foil and serve straight from the oven with slices of toasted baguette and endive salad.

PUDDINGS

BAKED VANILLA CHEESECAKE WITH STRAWBERRIES

SERVES 4

FOR THE STRAWBERRY SAUCE

STRAWBERRIES	500g, diced
CASTER SUGAR	20g
VANILLA POD	Seeds scraped from ½

FOR THE BASE

DIGESTIVE BISCUITS	100g
UNSALTED BUTTER	50g

FOR THE CHEESECAKE

FREE RANGE EGGS	2 medium
FREE RANGE EGG YOLKS	3 medium
CASTER SUGAR	180g
CREAM CHEESE	500g
DOUBLE CREAM	180ml
LEMON	1, zested and juiced
VANILLA POD	Seeds scraped from ½
CORNFLOUR	40g
ICING SUGAR	For dusting

For the biscuit base, firstly grease a 20cm flan case. Crush the digestive biscuits in a sealed plastic bag, so as not to lose any crumbs. Melt the butter in a saucepan. Add the crushed biscuits and stir. Cook for a couple of minutes. Remove from the heat and place in the prepared flan case. Pat the mixture down so it is compact. Refrigerate for about 30 minutes until set.

Pre-heat the oven to 180°C / gas mark 4.

Now make the cheesecake. In a bowl or food processor, whisk eggs, egg yolks and sugar until they've doubled in size. Add cream cheese, double cream, lemon juice and zest, vanilla seeds and cornflour and continue to whisk until firm. Be careful not to over whisk or the mixture will become runny again. Remove the base from the fridge and spoon the mixture on top. Bake for 20 minutes. Take out of the oven and gently remove the casing. Leave to cool.

For the strawberry sauce, place half the diced strawberries, sugar and vanilla seeds into a heavy-bottomed saucepan. Simmer gently until soft; this should take about 3 minutes. Remove from the heat and sieve into a bowl. Discard the pips. Leave to cool.

To serve, add the rest of the diced strawberries to the sauce and drizzle over the top of the cheesecake. Dust with icing sugar.

SPOTTED DICK WITH BUTTER, GOLDEN SYRUP AND CUSTARD

Serving spotted dick with a knob of butter on top and custard on the side is a tip from an old gentleman Tim Hughes once met on a train. Intrigued, we tried it, and sure enough, it was delicious. We serve it with butter to this day.

SERVES 4

PLAIN FLOUR	240g
BAKING POWDER	1 tsp
SALT	Pinch
SUET	120g
SOFT LIGHT BROWN SUGAR	80g
CURRANTS	120g
LEMON	½, grated
MIXED SPICE	½ tsp
WATER	200ml approximately
UNSALTED BUTTER	50g
GOLDEN SYRUP	4 tbsp
CUSTARD (*SEE PAGE 266*)	300ml

Sieve the flour and baking powder together into a large mixing bowl with the salt. Add suet, sugar, currants, lemon zest and mixed spice, and just enough water to make a soft dough. Mix together with your hands.

Put the dough into a greased 1 litre pudding basin. Drop into a steamer over boiling water. Cover the saucepan and cook for 1 ½ hours ensuring the pan doesn't boil dry. Top up with boiling water if necessary.

Remove wrappings and cut the pudding into 4cm slices. Place flat on each plate and serve with a knob of butter and drizzle with golden syrup, with custard on the side.

For this dish, we use a vegetable steamer sitting over a saucepan but you could use a colander.

CHOCOLATE AND CLEMENTINE TART

A refined, restaurant-style take on the classic pairing of chocolate and orange.

SERVES 6

CHOCOLATE (**70%** COCOA)	150g
UNSALTED BUTTER	100g, diced
FREE RANGE EGGS	3 medium
FREE RANGE EGG YOLKS	2 medium
CASTER SUGAR	30g
CLEMENTINES	4, finely grated
CREME FRAICHE	200ml

FOR THE SWEET PASTRY

UNSALTED BUTTER	150g, softened
CASTER SUGAR	140g
FREE RANGE EGGS	2 medium, beaten
PLAIN FLOUR	300g
BUTTER	For greasing

> To segment an orange without pith, top and tail the fruit with a knife. Running the knife along the contours of the orange, remove the peel and pith. Cut in between each segment, freeing up the flesh.

Firstly make the pastry. In a bowl or food processor, gently mix butter and sugar together until combined. Slowly add eggs until thoroughly mixed. Sieve in the flour and slowly mix until a smooth dough is formed. Wrap in Clingfilm and store in the fridge until required. The pastry must be rested for at least 2 hours before use.

Pre-heat the oven to 180°C / gas mark 4.

On a floured surface, roll out the pastry to about ½cm thickness. Grease a 23cm flan case with a little butter and carefully lay the rolled pastry over it, ensuring you press the sides well and there are no air pockets or holes in the pastry. Cover the pastry base with a ring of baking paper, place baking beans (or rice) on top and bake for 15 minutes. Remove from the oven. The pastry should feel slightly dry to the touch and be golden brown in colour. Allow to cool.

Turn the oven down to 140°C / gas mark 1.

Meanwhile, break the chocolate into small pieces. Add to the butter in a heat-proof bowl and melt over a boiling water bath (bain-marie), stirring occasionally. This should take no more than 5 minutes. Once melted, remove the bowl from the heat. In another bowl or food processor, whisk eggs, egg yolks and sugar until they've doubled in size. Carefully fold in the chocolate mixture. Add the clementine zest and pour into the flan case. Bake for 10 minutes until set, remove from the oven and leave to cool.

FOR THE COMPOTE

CLEMENTINE	1, juiced
SEEDLESS CLEMENTINES (*SEE OPPOSITE*)	4, segmented
CASTER SUGAR	1 tbsp

For the compote, pour the clementine juice into a small saucepan and add the sugar. Gently heat until the sugar dissolves and the juice starts to thicken. Add the clementine segments and remove from the heat.

Slice the tart and serve with a spoonful of compote and crème fraîche.

ROASTED PEACHES WITH ICED LIME CREME FRAICHE

SERVES 4

PEACHES	4
SOFT DARK BROWN SUGAR	50g
AMARETTI BISCUITS	50g, crushed
UNSALTED BUTTER	50g
AMARETTO (*SWEET WINE OR MARSALA WOULD BE GOOD ALTERNATIVES*)	Splash

FOR THE ICED LIME CREME FRAICHE

LIMES	5, zested and juiced
ICING SUGAR	180g
CREME FRAICHE	450g
WATER	90ml

For the iced lime crème fraîche, thoroughly combine the lime juice, zest, water and sieved icing sugar in a bowl. Leave to stand for 30 minutes to develop the flavours. Mix the lime water into the crème fraîche. Pour into a container and freeze for up to 3 hours until firm.

Pre-heat the oven to 170°C / gas mark 3.

Halve the peaches, remove stones and place the fruit flesh-side up in an oven-proof dish. Sprinkle the peaches with sugar, crushed Amaretti biscuits, a knob of butter on each and douse with Amaretto. Bake for approximately 10 minutes until the peaches are cooked and the juices are bubbling and syrupy.

To serve, place the peaches onto 4 plates. Drizzle over the cooking juices and serve with curls of iced lime crème fraîche.

BENI WILD HARVEST CHOCOLATE POT WITH BLOOD ORANGE

Opinion is divided on the provenance of blood oranges, which may have originated in China or the southern Mediterranean. We favour Sicilian blood oranges in season, from January through to March, available from good greengrocers, specialist stores and most supermarkets. They are sometimes known as 'ruby' to protect the squeamish. Beni Wild Harvest has a 66% cocoa content made from wild Bolivian cocoa by the Original Beans company. Another chocolate with a similar cocoa level would also work.

SERVES 4

FOR THE CHOCOLATE POTS

FREE RANGE EGG YOLKS	4 medium
CASTER SUGAR	90g
WHIPPING CREAM	190ml
MILK	190ml
BENI WILD HARVEST CHOCOLATE	125g, broken into pieces

FOR THE COMPOTE

BLOOD ORANGE	3 (1 juiced; 2 grated and segmented)
CASTER SUGAR	1 tbsp
GRAND MARNIER	Splash

For the chocolate pots, mix the egg yolks and sugar together in a bowl. In a heavy-bottomed saucepan bring the cream, milk and orange zest gently to the boil, remove from the heat, add the chocolate pieces and stir until all the chocolate has melted.

Add the egg and sugar mixture to the chocolate and cream and stir well. Return it to the stove and cook on a low heat – do not allow to boil – stirring continuously until the mixture coats the back of a spoon. This should take about 3 minutes. Pour into pots or ramekins and allow to set in the refrigerator for a couple of hours (alternatively, do this the night before).

To make the compote, pour the blood orange juice into a small saucepan and add the sugar. Gently heat until the sugar dissolves and the juice starts to thicken. Add the blood orange segments, a splash of Grand Marnier, stir well and remove from heat.

Remove the chocolate pots from the fridge. Spoon the blood orange compote on top of the ramekins and decorate with chocolate curls.

Use a peeler to make chocolate curls and peel over each pot.

RASPBERRY AND ELDERFLOWER TRIFLE

Probably the quintessential British pudding. The first recipe for a cream trifle appears in 1596 in Thomas Dawson's *The Good Huswifes Jewell,* but the classic dessert as we know it with wine-soaked biscuits and custard appears in the eighteenth century. *Mrs Beeton's Book of Household Management* (1861) has no less than four recipes and it is here, in the Victorian era, that trifle really takes hold, whether with booze in London gentlemen's clubs or without for children's parties. Ours is a more modern twist with raspberries and raspberry liqueur while retaining jelly and custard.

SERVES 4

FOR THE SPONGE

FREE RANGE EGGS	4 medium
CASTER SUGAR	90g
PLAIN FLOUR	70g

FOR THE CUSTARD
(yields approximately 200ml)

CASTER SUGAR	30g
FREE RANGE EGG YOLKS	4 medium
DOUBLE CREAM	200ml
VANILLA POD	Seeds scraped from ½

FOR THE JELLY

GELATINE	2 leaves
WHITE WINE	200ml
ELDERFLOWER CORDIAL	65ml
RASPBERRIES	65g
CASTER SUGAR	40g

FOR THE MERINGUE

CASTER SUGAR	75g
FREE RANGE EGG WHITES	2

Pre-heat the oven to 110°C / gas mark ¼. For the meringue, line a baking tray with greaseproof paper. In a bowl or food processor, whisk the egg whites and sugar until it forms stiff peaks. Pipe the mixture into small classic meringue shapes on the greaseproof paper. Bake for about 40 minutes until the meringue is crisp and dry. Remove from the oven and allow to cool.

For the sponge, turn up the oven to 180°C / gas mark 4. In a bowl or food processor, whisk the eggs and sugar until doubled in size. Sieve the flour and gently fold into the egg mixture. Spread evenly to 2cm thickness onto a greaseproof paper-lined baking tray and bake in the oven for 6 to 8 minutes.

To make the custard, beat together the sugar and egg yolks in a bowl. In a thick-bottomed saucepan, bring the cream and vanilla seeds to the boil. Remove from the heat, pour immediately onto the egg mixture and whisk together. Return to the pan and over a gentle heat stir continuously with a wooden spoon until the custard coats the back of the spoon. Ensure you don't boil the custard, as it will scramble. The consistency should be thick. Sieve the custard into a bowl, and place it on top of a larger bowl of iced water to cool. Once cool, cover with Clingfilm and refrigerate until needed.

FOR THE WHIPPED CREAM	
DOUBLE CREAM	300ml
ELDERFLOWER CORDIAL	1 tbsp

FOR THE RASPBERRY SAUCE	
RASPBERRIES	100g
CASTER SUGAR	25g
WATER	30ml
LEMON	Squeeze

FOR ASSEMBLING THE TRIFLE	
RASPBERRY LIQUEUR	50ml
RASPBERRIES	100g
FRESH ELDERFLOWERS (IF AVAILABLE)	For decoration

For the jelly, cover the gelatine with cold water in a bowl and soak until soft. Meanwhile, heat the white wine, elderflower cordial, raspberries and sugar in a saucepan for about 3 minutes until the fruit has softened. Drain the gelatine and add it to the raspberry mixture. Stir well until the gelatine has dissolved. Strain into a bowl, discarding the raspberry pips and set aside.

For the raspberry sauce, liquidise the raspberries, sugar, water and lemon juice until smooth. Pass through a strainer.

To assemble the trifle, cut the sponge into 2cm square pieces and place in a large glass trifle bowl. Soak with the raspberry liqueur. Place most of the raspberries on top (keeping back a few for decoration) and cover with elderflower and raspberry jelly. Refrigerate until set; this should take at least 2 hours.

Prepare the whipped cream by whipping together the cream and elderflower cordial until it forms soft peaks. Break up some of the meringues and add them to the whipped cream.

Top the set jelly with the custard, then the cream and meringue mixture. Toss the remaining raspberries in the sauce and drizzle over the top. Decorate with fresh elderflowers and the remaining meringues.

STEAMED CHOCOLATE AND MARMALADE SPONGE PUDDING WITH CUSTARD

Steamed pudding and custard, a perfect British dessert.

SERVES 4

SEVILLE ORANGE THICK-CUT MARMALADE	120g
DARK CHOCOLATE (70% COCOA)	80g
UNSALTED BUTTER	100g
CASTER SUGAR	100g
FREE RANGE EGGS	2 medium, beaten
PLAIN FLOUR	80g
COCOA POWDER	20g
BAKING POWDER	1 tsp
ORANGE	1, finely grated
CUSTARD (SEE PAGE 266)	300ml
CHOCOLATE SAUCE (SEE PAGE 274)	280ml

Grease a 1 litre pudding basin with butter and spoon 80g of the marmalade into the bottom of the basin (keeping back a tablespoon's worth for garnish).

Break 50g of the chocolate into small pieces in a heat-proof bowl and melt over a boiling water bath (bain-marie), stirring occasionally. This should take no more than 5 minutes.

In a bowl or food processor, cream the butter and sugar together. Slowly add the beaten eggs. Sieve the flour, cocoa powder and baking powder into the mixture. Fold in the melted chocolate and the orange zest, mix well and spoon into the pudding basin.

Break the remaining 30g of chocolate into small pieces and, using your fingers, insert into the middle of the pudding. Drop into a steamer (see page 258) over boiling water. Cover the saucepan and cook for an hour, ensuring the pan doesn't boil dry. Top up with boiling water if necessary.

Turn the pudding out onto a warm serving plate. In a small saucepan gently heat the rest of the marmalade with an equal amount of water and pour over the top of the pudding. Serve with custard and chocolate sauce.

DORSET BLUEBERRY SOUFFLE WITH RIPPLE ICE CREAM

Thanks to a tendency to sandy acidic soil, Dorset was home to the first commercial blueberry-growing company in Britain. The bushes also grow well in pots. If you cannot source British blueberries in season, then look for fruit from elsewhere in Europe (maybe labelled 'myrtle') and perhaps avoid the carbon footprint of fruit flown in from Peru.

SERVES 4

FOR THE SOUFFLES

BLUEBERRIES	150g
UNSALTED BUTTER	40g, softened, with extra for greasing
PLAIN FLOUR	30g
MILK	125ml
ICING SUGAR	15g, with extra for dusting
SALT	Pinch
FREE RANGE EGGS	5 medium, separated
CASTER SUGAR	50g, with extra for dusting
CORNFLOUR	15g

FOR THE BLUEBERRY SAUCE

BLUEBERRIES	150g
CASTER SUGAR	50g
WATER	60ml

FOR THE RIPPLE ICE CREAM

VANILLA ICE CREAM (*SEE PAGE 274*)	½ litre
BLUEBERRY SAUCE	3 tbsp

For the blueberry sauce, put the blueberries, sugar and water in a saucepan and bring to the boil. Simmer for about 5 minutes, or until the blueberries are soft. Press the cooked fruit through a sieve into a bowl, discarding the skins and pips. Set aside until needed.

Now prepare the ice cream. If using home-made ice cream, after churning and before freezing, fold in half the blueberry sauce to create a ripple effect. If using ready-made ice cream, remove from the freezer, allow to soften for half an hour, fold in half the blueberry sauce and re-freeze.

For the soufflés, pre-heat the oven to 200ºC / gas mark 6 and grease 4 ramekins or small oven-proof bowls with butter and dust with caster sugar.

Liquidise 125g blueberries to a fine purée. Keep to one side.

In a mixing bowl, combine the butter and flour into a paste. In a saucepan, bring the milk and blueberry purée to the boil. Add the paste, whisking continuously until smooth. Bring back to the boil and simmer for 3 minutes.

In a separate bowl, mix the sieved icing sugar, salt and egg yolks. Whisk into the hot blueberry mixture, and simmer for another 2 minutes. Pour into a bowl and leave to cool.

Whisk the egg whites, sugar and cornflour together until stiff and dry. Add half of this to the blueberry mixture and beat vigorously. Gently fold in the rest of the whisked egg whites.

Half fill your prepared ramekins with the soufflé mixture. Divide the remaining 25g blueberries and place a small handful into the middle of each. Fill to the top with more soufflé mixture. Using a palate knife, smooth the top until flush with the ramekin. Make a slight indentation with your thumb around the edge. This will allow the soufflé to rise and prevent it from snagging. Bake in the pre-heated oven for 12 minutes.

When the soufflés have risen, remove from the oven. Dust with icing sugar. Place on a plate and, at the last minute, make a small incision in the soufflé with a teaspoon and pour in the rest of the blueberry sauce. Serve with the ripple ice cream.

BAKED CHOCOLATE PUDDING WITH MINT CHOCOLATE CHIP ICE CREAM

SERVES 4

FOR THE MINT CHOCOLATE CHIP ICE CREAM

VANILLA ICE CREAM (*IF USING HOME-MADE ICE CREAM (SEE PAGE 274) IT'S BEST TO MAKE IT THE DAY BEFORE*)	500ml
CREME DE MENTHE	Splash
MINT (*IF USING HOME-MADE ICE CREAM*)	½ small bunch
DARK CHOCOLATE CHIPS	100g

FOR THE CHOCOLATE PUDDING

FREE RANGE EGGS	2 medium
FREE RANGE EGG YOLKS	3 medium
CASTER SUGAR	50g
DARK CHOCOLATE (70% COCOA)	200g
UNSALTED BUTTER	75g, diced
PLAIN FLOUR	40g, sieved
BUTTER	For greasing
ICING SUGAR	For dusting

If using home-made ice cream, before churning the vanilla ice cream base, mix in the fresh mint leaves and leave in the fridge overnight. Next day, sieve to remove the mint, add a splash of Crème de Menthe and churn as normal. Add the chocolate chips after churning and freeze.

If using ready-made ice cream, remove it from the freezer, allow to soften for half an hour, mix in a splash of Crème de Menthe and chocolate chips and re-freeze.

Pre-heat the oven to 190ºC / gas mark 5.

In a bowl or food processor, whisk eggs, egg yolks and sugar until they've doubled in size. Meanwhile, break the chocolate into small pieces. Put the butter into a heat-proof bowl, add the chocolate pieces and melt over a boiling water bath (bain-marie), stirring occasionally. This should take no more than 5 minutes.

Once the chocolate has melted, remove the bowl from the heat and stir its contents into the egg and sugar mixture. Fold in the flour and mix well. Spoon the mixture into 4 small buttered baking dishes and cook for 8 minutes.

Remove the chocolate puddings from the oven, dust with icing sugar and serve with mint chocolate chip ice cream.

HONEYCOMB ICE CREAM WITH HOT CHOCOLATE SAUCE

The inspiration for our honeycomb ice cream came from one of our Australian chefs about a decade ago and has proved to be a favourite ever since, never straying far from the original recipe.

SERVES 4

FOR THE HONEYCOMB

CASTER SUGAR	200g
LIQUID GLUCOSE	25g
BICARBONATE OF SODA	1 tsp
COLD WATER	60ml

FOR THE ICE CREAM
(yields around 1 litre)

FREE RANGE EGG YOLKS	12 medium
CASTER SUGAR	190g
MILK	500ml
DOUBLE CREAM	375ml
VANILLA POD	Seeds scraped from 1
WHITE CHOCOLATE	100g, frozen and finely grated
HONEYCOMB	½, crushed

FOR THE CHOCOLATE SAUCE
(yields around 560ml)

DOUBLE CREAM	250ml
MILK	60ml
CHOCOLATE (55% COCOA)	250g

To make the honeycomb, place sugar, glucose and water in a large heavy-bottomed saucepan and heat until the mixture starts to caramelise. Ensure that no sugar is left to crystallise on the sides of the pan by brushing down with a wet pastry brush.

Remove the caramel from the heat, and whisk in bicarbonate of soda. It will dramatically bubble up and be very hot, so be extra careful. Pour the hot, foamy mixture onto a large piece of greaseproof paper and spread out thinly with a palette knife. Leave to cool for 20 minutes. Once cool, break half the honeycomb into shards for garnishing, and crush the rest for the ice cream.

For the ice cream, in a bowl or food processor, whisk egg yolks and sugar until doubled in size. In a heavy-bottomed saucepan, bring the milk, cream, vanilla pod and seeds to the boil. Remove from the heat, lift out the vanilla pod and pour onto the egg mixture. Sieve into a bowl and chill before churning in an ice cream maker. Once the ice cream has been churned, it can either be turned out into a container and frozen as vanilla ice cream or more ingredients can be added at this stage, before freezing, while the ice cream is still soft. Gently fold in the grated white chocolate and crushed honeycomb. Freeze for at least 2 hours.

For the chocolate sauce, pour cream and milk into a heavy-bottomed saucepan and bring to the boil. Break the chocolate into small pieces and put in a heat-proof bowl. Pour the hot cream and milk over and stir until all the chocolate has dissolved.

Serve the ice cream in coupe or cocktail glasses, topped with honeycomb shards and hot chocolate sauce.

MASCARPONE AND WHITE CHOCOLATE ICE CREAM WITH WARM SUMMER FRUITS

This recipe is a variation on the theme of one of our most iconic dishes: Scandinavian iced berries with hot white chocolate sauce.

SERVES 4

FOR THE WARM SUMMER FRUITS

STRAWBERRIES	100g
CASTER SUGAR	75g
WATER	50ml
SUMMER FRUITS (*WILD STRAWBERRIES, RASPBERRIES, BLUEBERRIES, BLACKBERRIES*)	400g

FOR THE MASCARPONE AND WHITE CHOCOLATE ICE CREAM

WHITE CHOCOLATE	100g
MILK	200ml
CREAM	100ml
FREE RANGE EGG YOLKS	5 medium
CASTER SUGAR	100g
MASCARPONE	100g

If using ready-made ice cream (½ litre), remove from the freezer, allow to soften for half an hour, mix in the white chocolate shards and re-freeze.

For the white chocolate shards, break the chocolate into small pieces in a heat-proof bowl and melt over a boiling water bath (bain-marie), stirring occasionally. This should take no more than 5 minutes. Once melted, spread thinly onto a greaseproof-lined tray – no more than 2mm thickness – and place in the fridge for 20 minutes until it's hard.

For the ice cream, boil the cream and milk in a heavy-bottomed saucepan. In a bowl or food processor, whisk the egg yolks and sugar until doubled in size. Whisk the boiling milk and cream into the egg mixture and allow to cool for a few minutes.

Add the mascarpone, whisking well to stop lumps from forming. Sieve into a bowl and place in the fridge to cool. Once cool, churn in an ice cream maker. When the churning process has finished, remove the white chocolate from the fridge, break into small shards and mix into the ice cream before placing in the freezer, retaining some chocolate shards for decoration. Freeze for at least 2 hours.

Prepare the warm summer fruits. In a saucepan, bring the strawberries, sugar and water to a boil. Simmer until the strawberries are soft, around 3 minutes. Strain the juice into a bowl, discarding the cooked strawberries. Add the summer fruits to the strawberry juice.

To serve, warm the summer fruit mixture in a pan, being careful not to boil. Sprinkle the remaining chocolate shards into bowls and spoon in 2 generous scoops of ice cream. Top with warmed summer fruits.

TWINKLE JELLY WITH AMALFI LEMON ICE CREAM AND CANDIED LEMON

Grown on the hills of Campania in Italy, sweet Amalfi lemons are at their peak in summer and available in the UK from good greengrocers, specialist stores and some supermarkets. Gold leaf can be found online. For this dish prepare the ice cream the day before.

SERVES 4

FOR THE JELLY

GELATINE	3½ leaves
PROSECCO	300ml
CASTER SUGAR	100g
ELDERFLOWER CORDIAL	25ml
VODKA	75ml
GOLD LEAF	1 sheet (available online)

FOR THE AMALFI LEMON ICE CREAM

VANILLA ICE CREAM (*SEE PAGE 274*)	1 litre
AMALFI LEMONS	2, finely grated and juiced
LIMONCELLO (*OPTIONAL*)	1 tbsp

FOR THE CANDIED LEMON

UNWAXED LEMON	1, zest removed with a potato peeler and thinly sliced lengthways
CASTER SUGAR	50g

To prepare the candied lemon, place the sliced zest in a small saucepan, cover with water and bring to the boil. Strain the zest and plunge into cold water. Repeat this process 3 times. Pat dry with kitchen roll and mix into the sugar. This will keep for up to a week in an airtight container.

Prepare the lemon ice cream the day before. See page 274 for the vanilla ice cream base. Before churning, mix in the zest, juice and limoncello, and churn as normal and freeze. If using ready-made vanilla ice cream, remove from the freezer, allow to soften for half an hour, mix in zest, juice and limoncello and re-freeze.

For the jelly, cover the gelatine with cold water in a bowl and soak until soft. Meanwhile, in a saucepan, heat the prosecco with the sugar until it has dissolved. Remove from the heat. Drain the gelatine and add it to the prosecco mixture. Stir well until the gelatine has dissolved. Add the elderflower cordial, vodka and gold leaf and mix well. Pour into individual jelly moulds and place in the fridge until set. This should take 4 hours.

To make the lemon curd, bring the lemon juice to the boil in a saucepan. Immediately remove from the heat. In a bowl, mix the sugar and egg and add to the lemon juice. Return the saucepan to a medium heat and whisk continuously for about 5 minutes until the liquid begins to simmer. Remove from the heat and slowly whisk in the butter. Sieve into a bowl, cover with Clingfilm and refrigerate.

LEMONS	5, juiced
CASTER SUGAR	50g
FREE RANGE EGG	1 medium
UNSALTED BUTTER	40g

To serve, dip the jelly moulds in a bowl of just-boiled water to loosen the jelly and turn out onto 4 plates. Spread the lemon curd to the side of the jelly and serve with a scoop of Amalfi lemon ice cream, topped with candied lemon.

GOOSEBERRY CRUMBLE

A summer dish for gooseberry season, but of course good with any seasonal fruit – classic apples or plums in autumn, forced Yorkshire rhubarb in winter.

SERVES 4

FOR CRUMBLE TOPPING

UNSALTED BUTTER	125g, softened
PLAIN FLOUR	250g
FREE RANGE EGG	½, beaten
SOFT BROWN SUGAR	100g

FOR GOOSEBERRY COMPOTE

UNSALTED BUTTER	25g
GOOSEBERRIES	400g, topped and tailed
CASTER SUGAR	50g
ELDERFLOWER CORDIAL	20ml

Pre-heat the oven to 180°C / gas mark 4.

For the crumble topping, place butter, flour, egg and sugar into a mixing bowl and gently rub with your fingers until you have a fine breadcrumb consistency. Place to one side until the compote is ready.

For the gooseberry compote, melt the butter in a saucepan and add the gooseberries, stirring for 5 minutes until they have softened a little. Add the sugar and elderflower cordial and remove from the heat. Pour the mixture into separate oven-proof dishes and top with crumble mix.

Bake for 12–15 minutes until golden brown.

Serve with Jersey cream, clotted cream or custard (see page 266).

PEACH MELBA PAVLOVA

A harmonious blending of two classic desserts, both created to honour artists – peach Melba by Escoffier at the Savoy for Australian soprano Dame Nellie Melba and Pavlova named after Russian ballet dancer Anna Pavlova. Created by our group pastry chef Phil Usher.

SERVES 4

FOR THE MERINGUE

SUNFLOWER OIL	For brushing
FREE RANGE EGG WHITES	2 medium
CASTER SUGAR	90g
VANILLA POD	Seeds scraped from ½
CORNFLOUR	½ tsp
HOT WATER	20ml
WHITE WINE VINEGAR	1 tsp

FOR THE TOPPING

RASPBERRIES	150g
CASTER SUGAR	20g
WATER	30ml
LEMON	Squeeze
VANILLA ICE CREAM (*SEE PAGE 274*)	½ litre
RIPE PEACH	1, sliced
ICING SUGAR	For dusting

Pre-heat the oven to 110°C / gas mark ¼.

Line a baking tray with greaseproof paper and spray or brush with a thin layer of sunflower oil.

For the meringue, place egg whites, sugar, vanilla and cornflour into a bowl or food processor and whisk until the mixture forms soft peaks. In a saucepan, warm through the water and vinegar, remove from the heat and, while whisking, gradually add to the egg white mix. Continue to mix for a further 3 minutes until it forms stiff peaks.

Using an 8cm metal ring or cutter to shape the meringues, place on the baking tray and pipe in the mixture until three quarters full. Dip the ring in hot water each time to clean and prevent the mixture from sticking. Bake in the oven for an hour and a half until the meringues are crisp and dry. Remove from the oven and allow to cool.

Liquidise 100g raspberries, sugar, water and lemon juice until smooth. Pass through a strainer and discard the pips.

When ready to serve, place the meringues in the centre of each plate. Gently indent the middle of each meringue with your finger and add a spoonful of vanilla ice cream. Top with the peach slices and remaining raspberries, and finish with a drizzle of raspberry sauce. Finally, sprinkle with icing sugar.

BLACKBERRY POSSET WITH VANILLA SHORTBREAD

Posset, more often flavoured with citrus such as lemon or orange to cut through the cream, is a traditional British pudding, similar to syllabub. It works beautifully here with blackberries.

SERVES 4

FOR THE POSSET

GELATINE	1½ leaves
BLACKBERRIES	300g
DOUBLE CREAM	400ml
CASTER SUGAR	100g
LEMON	1, juiced

FOR THE VANILLA SHORTBREAD

SALTED BUTTER	125g, softened
CASTER SUGAR	60g
VANILLA POD	Seeds scraped from ½
PLAIN FLOUR	125g
CORNFLOUR	60g

Firstly prepare the posset, as it needs to be made the day before you plan to serve it. Cover the gelatine with cold water in a bowl and soak until soft.

Liquidise 250g blackberries to a fine purée. Take 2 tablespoons of the purée and set aside for when you serve the dish. Pour the rest of the purée into a saucepan with the cream, sugar and lemon juice. Bring to the boil and let it bubble for 3 minutes until it thickens. Remove from the heat and sieve into a bowl.

Remove the gelatine from the water and squeeze out excess water. Add the gelatine to the warm blackberry mixture and stir until it has dissolved. Pour into glass coupes and refrigerate overnight to set.

To make the shortbread, pre-heat the oven to 180ºC / gas mark 4 and line a large baking tray with greaseproof paper.

Mix butter, sugar and vanilla seeds in a bowl. Sieve in the flour and cornflour and mix until you have a smooth paste. Roll out on a floured surface to 1cm thickness. Cut into 2cm x 8cm rectangles and place on the prepared baking tray. Prick the dough at even intervals with a fork and bake for 6 to 8 minutes until light golden in colour. Leave to cool.

To serve, cut the remaining blackberries in half, mix them with the blackberry purée and spoon onto each glass of posset. Serve with a vanilla shortbread.

RIBSTON PIPPIN APPLE AND BLACKBERRY PIE

Ribston Pippin is an 'aromatic' apple originating from Ribston Hall in Yorkshire, widely thought to be the parent of the better known Cox's Orange Pippin. We sometimes substitute 300g stoned greengages and 300g stoned damsons for the apple and blackberry.

SERVES 4

FOR THE PASTRY

SALTED BUTTER	90g, softened
CASTER SUGAR	120g
PLAIN FLOUR	225g
BAKING POWDER	1½ tsp
SALT	Pinch
DOUBLE CREAM	100ml

FOR THE APPLE AND BLACKBERRY FILLING

RIBSTON PIPPIN APPLES (*COX OR BRAMLEY WOULD ALSO BE FINE*)	500g
UNSALTED BUTTER	50g, with extra for greasing
CASTER SUGAR	50g, with extra for dusting
LEMON	1, juiced
BLACKBERRIES	100g
PLAIN FLOUR	For dusting
FREE RANGE EGG WHITE	1 medium

To make the pastry, cream together butter and sugar in a bowl or food processor. Mix the sieved flour, baking powder and salt into the creamed butter and sugar. Add the double cream and mix to a smooth dough. Wrap the dough in Clingfilm and refrigerate. Allow to rest for at least 2 hours before rolling.

For the pie filling, peel, core and roughly dice the apples. Melt the butter in a heavy-bottomed saucepan. Add the sugar and half the chopped apples and cook for 5 minutes until they start to soften. Add the rest of the apples and the lemon juice and cook for a further 2 minutes. Remove from the heat, stir in the blackberries and leave to cool.

Pre-heat the oven to 180°C / gas mark 4 and grease a 20cm diameter pie dish with butter.

Roll three quarters of the pastry to ½cm thickness. Carefully lay the rolled pastry into the prepared dish, ensuring you press the sides well and there are no air pockets or holes in the pastry. Add the apple and blackberry filling. Cover with the rest of the pastry to form a lid and crimp the edges to seal. Cut a hole in the top to let out steam. Brush with the egg white and sprinkle with sugar.

Bake the pie for 20 minutes, or until golden brown. Remove from the oven and leave to cool for a few minutes before serving with a generous scoop of vanilla ice cream (see page 274), clotted cream or custard (see page 266).

WILLIAMS PEAR TARTS WITH CREME BRULEE ICE CREAM AND BUTTERSCOTCH SAUCE

SERVES 4

FOR THE CREME BRULEE ICE CREAM

VANILLA ICE CREAM BASE (*SEE PAGE 274*)	½ litre, unchurned
ICING SUGAR	100g

FOR THE BUTTERSCOTCH SAUCE

DOUBLE CREAM	150ml
SOFT DARK BROWN SUGAR	75g
SALTED BUTTER	15g

FOR THE TART

PUFF PASTRY	200g
PLAIN FLOUR	For dusting
PEARS	2 large ripe, cored and finely sliced lengthways
FREE RANGE EGG YOLK	1 medium
UNSALTED BUTTER	10g

FOR THE ALMOND CREAM

UNSALTED BUTTER	60g
CASTER SUGAR	60g
FREE RANGE EGG	1 medium, beaten
LEMON	Squeeze
BRANDY	1 tsp
GROUND ALMONDS	125g
PLAIN FLOUR	1 tbsp, sieved

For the crème brûlée ice cream, take the vanilla ice cream base and, before churning, pour it into a heat-proof dish and refrigerate, uncovered, until a skin develops on the surface (this shouldn't take more than a couple of hours). Make sure you don't have anything too powerfully flavoured in the fridge or it will taint the ice cream!

Remove the ice cream base from the fridge, dust heavily with sieved icing sugar and caramelise the sugar until golden either carefully using a blow torch or by placing it under a hot grill. Churn as usual and freeze for at least a couple of hours.

To make the butterscotch sauce, bring the cream and sugar to the boil in a saucepan. Reduce the heat and simmer for 5 minutes. Whisk in the butter. Remove from the heat. Cool and store in the fridge until required.

To make the tarts, start by lining a large baking tray with greaseproof paper.

For the almond cream, mix together the butter and sugar in a bowl or food processor. Slowly add the egg, mixing well. Add the lemon juice, brandy, ground almonds, flour and mix well. Set aside for later.

Lay the puff pastry on a floured surface. Roll to a thickness of 4mm and cut 4 circles with a diameter of 10cm (using a cutter or cut around a saucer). Place onto the baking tray and prick all over with a fork. Leave to rest for 1 hour.

Pre-heat the oven to 180°C / gas mark 4.

Spoon the almond cream mixture sparingly into the middle of the pastry discs. Top with pear slices, slightly overlapping each other, but not too close to the edge of the pastry. Leave a gap of about 1cm around the edge.

Melt the remaining butter in a pan and brush it over the pear slices. Brush egg yolk around the edge of the pastry. Bake the tarts for 12 to 15 minutes, until the pastry is cooked and has a golden brown colour.

Finally, gently re-heat the butterscotch sauce. Place the tarts on plates, drizzle with warm sauce, dust with icing sugar and serve with crème brûlée ice cream.

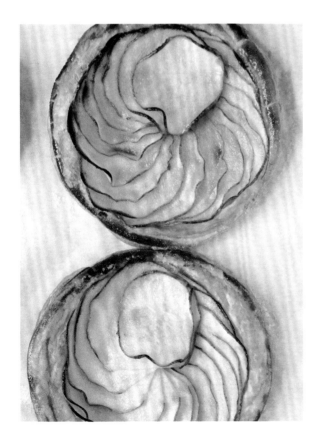

SAFFRON CUSTARD TART

Cornwall's love affair with saffron goes back, it is said, to Phoenician sailors trading it for tin. Elizabeth David in her classic *English Bread and Yeast Cookery* gives a recipe for a Cornish saffron cake, while warning against 'false, shameful saffron cakes' using substitutes. Sparingly used, this intensely aromatic spice makes for a delicious dessert. We love it here with custard.

SERVES 4

FOR THE SAFFRON CUSTARD FILLING

FREE RANGE EGGS	3 large
CASTER SUGAR	140g
SAFFRON STRANDS	Pinch
DOUBLE CREAM	250ml
MILK	250ml
VANILLA POD	Seeds scraped from ½
SWEET PASTRY (*SEE PAGE 260*)	

> If you place your empty blind-baked pastry case in the oven before pouring in the saffron custard, the level will be even and you won't have any spillage. However, be careful not to burn yourself.

Ideally make the saffron custard filling the day before to allow the saffron to infuse and improve the flavour. Begin by mixing the eggs and sugar together. Sprinkle the saffron strands into a saucepan with the cream, milk and vanilla seeds and bring to the boil. When boiling, remove from the heat, pour onto the egg mixture and whisk thoroughly. Cool at room temperature and refrigerate overnight.

Make the sweet pastry, see page 260.

Pre-heat the oven to 180°C / gas mark 4 and grease a 20cm flan case with a little butter.

On a floured surface, roll out the pastry to about 5mm thickness. Carefully lay the rolled pastry into the flan case, ensuring you press the sides well and there are no air pockets or holes in the pastry. Cover the pastry base with a ring of baking paper, place baking beans (or rice) on top and bake in the oven for 10 minutes. The pastry should feel slightly dry to the touch and be golden brown in colour. Allow to cool.

Turn the oven down to 130°C / gas mark ½.

To assemble the tart, sieve the saffron custard into a jug and pour into the tart case, filling it right to the top. Finely grate a little nutmeg across the surface. Bake in the oven until just set which should take about an hour. Remove from the oven, allow to cool and serve.

RICE PUDDING WITH ARMAGNAC PRUNES

Pruneaux à l'Armagnac, prunes soaked in Armagnac, are often served as an after-dinner treat in southwest France. Prepare the prunes the day before the rest of the dish.

SERVES 4

PUDDING RICE	60g
MILK	330ml
DOUBLE CREAM	160ml
VANILLA POD	Seeds scraped from ½
ORANGE	½, finely grated zest
UNSALTED BUTTER	40g
CONDENSED MILK	60ml
DEMERARA SUGAR	1 tbsp

FOR THE ARMAGNAC
PRUNES

AGEN PRUNES	200g
ARMAGNAC (OR BRANDY)	50ml

The day before making the pudding, stone the prunes and place in a bowl. Gently warm the Armagnac in a saucepan and pour over the fruit. Cover and store at room temperature until needed.

Wash the rice in cold water to remove excess starch. Bring the milk, cream, vanilla seeds and orange zest to the boil in a heavy-bottomed saucepan. Add the rice, reduce heat and simmer gently for around 30 minutes, stirring occasionally. When cooked, the rice should be soft and the mixture thick and creamy. Remove from the heat and stir in the butter and condensed milk.

Spoon the pudding into a heat-proof dish. Scatter with the demerara sugar and place under a hot grill until golden. Serve topped with Armagnac prunes.

YORKSHIRE RHUBARB AND BAKED CUSTARD

A native of Siberia, first imported here as a medicine, a vegetable classified by the US Customs court as a fruit, rhubarb, as we know it, took root here after 1817 when it was accidentally 'forced' (covered) at the Chelsea Physic Garden. At its height, the Rhubarb Triangle between Leeds, Wakefield and Bradford supplied Europe by nightly Rhubarb Express trains. Lack of sugar during the Second World War triggered a slow decline, but indoor Yorkshire rhubarb, still often harvested by candlelight, is an essential element of our winter menu and delicious here with a baked custard.

SERVES 4

FOR THE BAKED CUSTARD

CASTER SUGAR	75g
FREE RANGE EGG YOLKS	6 medium
DOUBLE CREAM	500ml
VANILLA POD	Seeds scraped from 1

FOR THE RHUBARB

YORKSHIRE RHUBARB	400g, chopped into 2cm pieces
CASTER SUGAR	100g

Pre-heat the oven to 150°C / gas mark 2.

In a bowl, beat together the sugar and egg yolks. In a thick-bottomed saucepan, bring the cream and vanilla seeds to the boil. Remove from the heat and pour immediately onto the egg mixture, whisking together. Sieve into a Pyrex dish. Place in a roasting tin. Fill the tin with warm water, being careful not to submerge the Pyrex dish. Place into the oven. Cook until set, around 50 minutes. Cool and then put into the fridge.

Now increase the oven temperature to 180°C / gas mark 4.

Spread the rhubarb out in a roasting dish. Sprinkle with the sugar and a splash of water. Cook for about 10 minutes until soft.

To serve, arrange the rhubarb on a plate and top with a large scoop of baked custard.

Put newspaper in the bottom
of the roasting tin to stop the Pyrex dish
from moving around.

CRU VIRUNGA CHOCOLATE CRACKLE BOMBE WITH WILD STRAWBERRIES

Cru Virunga is single-origin chocolate from Virunga National Park in war-torn eastern Congo. It is from the Original Beans company. For every 100g of chocolate purchased, a tree is planted in the country of origin, thus replenishing the natural habitats. If you cannot find it, substitute with a chocolate with 70% cocoa content. Popping candy and edible gold dust are widely available online and in some stores. Metal sphere moulds can be found in good kitchen shops and online. Alternatively, use small semi-circular plastic bowls.

SERVES 4

FOR THE ICE CREAM

VANILLA ICE CREAM (*SEE PAGE 274*)	½ litre
STRAWBERRY JAM	3 tbsp

FOR THE WILD STRAWBERRY COMPOTE

STRAWBERRIES	100g, diced
CASTER SUGAR	20g
VANILLA POD	Seeds scraped from ½
WILD STRAWBERRIES	50g

FOR THE CHOCOLATE SAUCE

DOUBLE CREAM	100ml
MILK	30ml
CRU VIRUNGA CHOCOLATE	50g
CHOCOLATE (70% COCOA)	50g

Firstly prepare the ice cream. If using home-made ice cream, after churning and before freezing, fold in the strawberry jam to create a ripple effect. If using ready-made ice cream, remove from the freezer, allow to soften for half an hour, fold in the strawberry jam and re-freeze.

For the wild strawberry compote, place the diced strawberries, sugar and vanilla seeds into a heavy-bottomed saucepan and simmer gently for around 3 minutes until soft. Remove from the heat, sieve into a bowl, discarding the pips, and add the wild strawberries. Leave to cool.

To make the chocolate sauce, pour the cream and milk into a heavy-bottomed saucepan and bring to the boil. Break the chocolate into small pieces and place in a heat-proof bowl. Pour the hot cream and milk over it and stir until all the chocolate has dissolved.

For the bombes, break the chocolate into small pieces, place in a heat-proof bowl and melt over a boiling water bath (bain-marie), stirring occasionally. This should take no more than 5 minutes. Once melted, remove from the heat, and place the bowl over a larger bowl of iced water to cool, but not set.

	FOR THE BOMBES
CRU VIRUNGA CHOCOLATE	400g
METAL HALF SPHERES	2 x 8cm, in diameter
CHOCOLATE POPPING CANDY	Small packet
EDIBLE GOLD DUST	Small packet

Brush the inside of each half sphere with the melted chocolate and refrigerate until firm. Repeat this process, adding a second coat. You may have to re-heat the chocolate mixture in the bowl so it remains soft enough. Return the moulds to the refrigerator. Once set, carefully remove the chocolate from each mould. For 4 people, you will need 8 of these. Refrigerate until ready to assemble the dish.

Pre-heat the oven to 180°C / gas mark 4. When ready to serve, heat a flat baking tray. With your hands, carefully pick up a chocolate half sphere and lightly hold the highest part of the dome against the hot tray for 5 seconds to melt the surface. Then stick it to the plate and allow it to set, so that it is firmly stuck on, like a chocolate bowl. Keep the baking tray hot.

Place a scoop of the rippled ice cream into each chocolate 'bowl'. Top with some of the strawberry compote and a pinch of popping candy. Again using the hot baking tray, quickly touch the rim of each of the other chocolate half spheres on the tray and attach to the plated half. Drizzle the remaining strawberry compote around the chocolate bombes.

Gently re-heat the chocolate sauce. Brush each bombe with edible gold dust, and place in front of your guests. Pour the hot chocolate sauce over the top.

DRINKS

BLOODY CAESAR

A delicious Bloody Mary with a briny hint of the sea. If Canada had an official mixed drink, this would be it: Canadians consume 350 million Bloody Caesars every year. Invented in 1969 at the Calgary Inn (now the Westin Hotel) in Calgary, Alberta, Restaurant Manager Walter Chell wanted to create a drink for the hotel's new Italian restaurant. Inspired by a pasta dish, spaghetti alle vongole, he combined vodka, tomato juice, clam broth, Worcestershire sauce, salt and pepper. Voila! A new twist on the classic Bloody was born. Legend has it that this drink inspired the invention of Clamato juice, which could be true. Chell ended up working for Mott's as Clamato's brand ambassador.

SERVES 1

LEMON	Wedge
CELERY SALT (*SEE PAGE 80*)	
LEMON	1, juiced
VODKA	50ml
CLAMATO JUICE	150ml
CELERY	1 stick , chopped in half lengthways and widthways

Wet the rim of a chilled highball glass with the lemon wedge, then dip the rim into celery salt. Pour in lemon juice and vodka. Add a pinch of celery salt and stir well. Fill with ice cubes and top up with Clamato juice. Stir again with a swizzle stick and garnish with a piece of celery.

BULL SHOT

J Sheekey regular Noël Coward's breakfast tipple: a richer, beefier, meatier twist on the classic Bloody Mary.

SERVES 1

LEMON	Wedge
CELERY SALT (*SEE PAGE 80*)	
LEMON	½, juiced
WORCESTERSHIRE SAUCE	1½ tbsp
VODKA	50ml
BEEF CONSOMME	150ml, room temperature
TABASCO	4 dashes
CELERY	1 stick , chopped in half lengthways and widthways

Wet the rim of a highball glass with the lemon wedge, then dip the rim in celery salt. Pour in the lemon juice, Worcestershire sauce and vodka. Add a pinch of celery salt and Tabasco. Stir well. Fill with ice cubes and then top up with beef consommé. Stir again with a swizzle stick. Garnish with a celery stick.

For a less beefy version (a Bloody Bull), mix with half beef consommé and half tomato juice.

BLOODY MARY

A number of people claim to have invented the Bloody Mary as we know it, from bartender Fernand Petiot at the New York Bar in 1921 to George Jessel in the late 1930s. However, minus the alcohol, the recipe arrived in 1872 in London from New York's Manhattan Club. Whatever its true history, the Bloody Mary is perfect as a lunchtime apéritif, especially at the weekend (though perhaps not the hangover cure that some people claim, except in its virgin form).

SERVES 1

LEMON	Wedge
CELERY SALT (*SEE PAGE 80*)	
LEMON	½, juiced
WORCESTERSHIRE SAUCE	1½ tbsp
HORSERADISH CREAM	1 tbsp
VODKA	50ml
TABASCO	4 dashes
TOMATO JUICE	150ml
CELERY	1 stick , chopped in half lengthways and widthways

Rub the rim of a highball glass with the lemon wedge, then dip the rim into celery salt. Pour in the lemon juice, Worcestershire sauce, horseradish cream, and vodka. Add a pinch of celery salt and Tabasco. Stir gently. Fill with ice cubes then top up with tomato juice. Stir again with a cocktail swizzle stick and garnish with a piece of celery.

Chill your highball glasses in the freezer first for perfect presentation.

PECHE D'AMOUR

Created in 2010 by Andy Gladding, one of
Sheekey's bartenders, this drink's bright fresh
fruit and surprising complexity have already
made it a timeless classic.

	SERVES 1
FRESH GINGER	1cm, peeled and finely chopped
VODKA	40ml
CREME DE PECHE	25ml
LIME	½, juiced
GINGER OR LIME	To garnish

Put the ginger into a cocktail shaker and muddle it.
Add the other ingredients, fill up with ice cubes and
shake hard for 30 seconds. Sieve into a cocktail glass
and serve straight up. Garnish with a fine slice of
ginger or a lime twist.

BLACK VELVET

Created by the bartender of the Brooks Club,
who described it as a 'Champagne in mourning'
to mark the death of Prince Albert in 1861. With
suitably sombre tones, this glorious layering of
Guinness and Champagne is the perfect match
for oysters. We serve a lot of Black Velvet in
J Sheekey Oyster Bar.

	SERVES 1
CHAMPAGNE	1 part
GUINNESS	1 part

This looks best in a silver or pewter tankard. First,
slowly pour in the Champagne. Then top up very
slowly with Guinness, otherwise it will overflow.

FISH HOUSE PUNCH

There's a little place just out of town,
Where, if you go to lunch,
They'll make you forget your mother-in-law
With a drink called Fish-House Punch
'The Cook' (1885)

Drinks don't get much more classic than this. Fish House Punch has been revered since 1732 when it was first concocted. Born at the Schuylkill Fishing Company, a Philadelphia fishing club and the oldest club in America, the drink takes its name from the association's riverside clubhouse, the Fish House. Already old when it was published in the first-ever cocktail book, Jerry Thomas's *How to Mix Drinks or The Bon-Vivant's Companion* (1862), it is sure to be around for centuries to come.

SERVES 1

DARK RUM	40ml
COGNAC VSOP	20ml
CREME DE PECHE	10ml
LEMON	½, juiced
SUGAR SYRUP	10ml
WATER	25ml
LEMON	Wedge

FOR THE SUGAR SYRUP

CASTER SUGAR	200g
WATER	200ml

First make the sugar syrup. It's worth making a small supply of this because it should last for up to 3 weeks when stored in the refrigerator. Fill a 200ml measure with sugar. Pour it into a bottle. Add 200ml water. Seal and shake the bottle for a few seconds. Shake again every 10 minutes until the sugar is dissolved. Refrigerate until ready to use.

Pour the rum, Cognac, crème de pêche, lemon juice, sugar syrup and water into a tumbler. Fill with ice cubes. Stir for 20 seconds. Garnish with the lemon wedge and serve.

NEGRONI

According to most accounts, the Negroni was invented in Florence, Italy, around 1919 at the Caffè Casoni. It was born as a variation on the most popular apéritif of the day, the Americano – a combination of Campari and sweet vermouth created by the inventor of Campari, Gaspare Campari, and originally named the Torino-Milano in tribute to the homes of its two ingredients. The Negroni takes its name from Count Camillo Negroni, an adventurer who had worked as a cowboy, banker and a riverboat gambler in the American west. During one visit to Caffè Casoni, Negroni asked the bartender, Fosco 'Gloomy' Scarselli, to add an extra touch to his Americano. He liked the drink, but wanted something stronger, so he asked Scarselli to replace the usual soda water with gin. As we write this, the Negroni family is shaking their family tree, certain it was not Count Camillo, but Pascal Olivier Count de Negroni who dreamt up this drink. Regardless of which Negroni it was, there's no denying it is one of the most delicious apéritifs ever created.

SERVES 1

CAMPARI	1 part
GIN	1 part
SWEET VERMOUTH SUCH AS CARPANO ANTICA FORMULA	1 part
ORANGE PEEL	Twist

Pour the Campari, gin and vermouth into a tumbler. Fill with ice cubes. Stir well. Garnish with a large orange twist and serve.

Use a potato peeler to cut the orange twist. To release extra orange flavour into the drink, squeeze the twist above the glass before dropping it in.

SAKE SOUR

This cocktail was created a couple of years ago by one of our bartenders, Simon Klapetek, at one of our in-house competitions. The theme was sake. His Sake Sour has a truly moreish, plummy flavour and has been on the menu ever since. Umeshu is a Japanese plum liqueur available in specialist drinks stores or online. Otherwise, use any plum liqueur.

SERVES 1

LEMON	½, juiced
UMESHU	50ml
SUGAR SYRUP (SEE PAGE 305)	10ml
FREE RANGE EGG WHITE	1 medium
GRIOTTE CHERRIES	3

Squeeze the lemon juice into a cocktail shaker. Add the Umeshu, sugar syrup and egg white. Shake hard, without ice, for about 40 seconds until the egg white emulsifies and froths. Top up the shaker with ice cubes and shake again for 20 seconds. Serve straight up (without ice) or on ice, according to preference. If using ice, serve in a tumbler. Straight up should be served in a Martini glass. At J Sheekey, we use old-fashioned American Martini glasses that look more like sherry glasses. In both cases, garnish with 3 griotte cherries on a cocktail stick.

Luxardo maraschino cherries are similar to griotte cherries and nothing like the bright red artificial maraschino cherries. If neither are available, use a fresh cherry and a drop or two of maraschino liqueur.

ALHAMBRA

This prize-winning cocktail was created by ex-J Sheekey bartender Maria Crowe at an in-house competition in collaboration with Sipsmith Independent Spirits. The beautiful Dame-Jeanne (glass amphora) Sipsmith awarded to Maria for this now resides in Sheekey's cellar.

SERVES 1

LEMON	½, juiced
SIPSMITH LONDON DRY (OR OTHER PREMIUM GIN)	50ml
MANZANILLA (OR OTHER DRY SHERRY)	10ml
LBV (LATE BOTTLED VINTAGE) PORT	10ml
SUGAR SYRUP (SEE PAGE 305)	10ml
ORANGE BITTERS	Dash
ORANGE PEEL	Twist

Squeeze the lemon juice into a cocktail shaker. Add the gin, sherry, port, sugar syrup and orange bitters. Fill the shaker with ice cubes and shake for 20 seconds. Strain into a Martini glass. Garnish with an orange twist.

MARTINI

This is the quintessential cocktail, which journalist H L Mencken called 'the only American invention as perfect as the sonnet'. Recipes vary on the ideal ratio of vermouth to gin or vodka. Heated debates have also been waged as to whether a Martini should be 'shaken, not stirred'. Noël Coward held that a Martini should be made by 'filling a glass with gin, then waving it in the general direction of Italy'. However, exhaustive taste-tests in the 1950s determined a ratio of 3.5:1 is the ideal formula. At J Sheekey, we have adapted this somewhat to the dryer palate. Crucial to the quality of the J Sheekey Martini is the quality of the gin, vodka and vermouth that we use. We urge you to use the finest you can afford and always use fresh vermouth (it is a wine and can spoil over time).

SERVES 1

PREMIUM GIN OR VODKA	75ml
DRY VERMOUTH	5ml
GREEN OLIVES (*OR A TWIST OF LEMON*)	2

Chill a Martini glass in the freezer for 10 minutes. Fill up a cocktail shaker with ice cubes. Add the gin or vodka and dry vermouth. Stir vigorously for 30 seconds to chill and slightly dilute the drink. Pour into the chilled Martini glass and serve straight up with 2 green olives or a lemon twist.

If you keep your vermouth in the fridge, it will last for 3 months. If you don't, it will go sour within a week!

For a Dirty Martini, add a little juice from the olive jar (according to taste), along with 2 olives. For a 'Gibson', swap the olives for 3 silver-skinned cocktail onions.

WINE

Making the right choice of wine for fish can be a fearful process for many afraid of making an unsuspecting gaff, or hung up by memories of the scene in From Russia With Love when Sean Connery's Bond spots Robert Shaw for a spectre goon by his ordering a Chianti to accompany grilled sole. There are no golden rules to matching fish with wine. It doesn't have to be a complicated or nuanced decision process, although there are some pairings that bring out the best in both. The key is to match the intensity of flavours in the food with the weight and personality of the wine, with neither overpowering the other.

An under-appreciated Picpoul de Pinet from the Coteaux du Languedoc sits well with oysters, and a classic white Burgundy has the right roundness for Sheekey's fish pie, but let's not write off reds and rosés. Indeed, there are as many reds as whites on Sheekey's list.

A dry rosé has its place alongside Mediterranean dishes, and is a good foil for our bisque and Cornish fish stew, both of which take culinary hints from the Med, rich with saffron and Cognac. Acidic reds, such as Barbera d'Alba from Piedmont, balance tomato-based dishes, and a light Pinot Noir works with salmon and red mullet, avoiding the metallic taste robust reds bring out in meaty fish. As the flavours build, so should the wines. Anchovies need a savoury Mediterranean red or a chilled Fino sherry to cut through the salt and oiliness.

Crisp, refreshing whites are great palate cleansers. The acidity found in Champagne and sparkling wines works especially well with squid tempura and classic fish and chips, while a tart Loire Sauvignon, good Portuguese Vinho Verde or young white Rioja will match the omega fats of mackerel. For spiced fish dishes, pick something simple, dry and friendly, such as a Gavi or Pinot Grigio or their near cousins, Riesling and Pinot Gris, which also work well with smoked salmon.

For most shellfish, turn to unoaked Chardonnay or Pinot Blanc, though mussels, for instance, are fine with an inexpensive dry white such as Muscadet. Scallops work best with wines that carry a little sweetness, such as Chenin Blanc from the Loire. Crab salad and German Riesling are a perfect match, though Meursault or Champagne work well, too. Light- to medium-bodied unoaked white wines, like Chablis, Riesling and Albariño, also have pure, positive flavours and a vivid acidity that complement the salt in shellfish.

If baking or poaching a fish, serve a better wine, and, if cooking in a rich creamy sauce, drink the best your budget allows. Firm white fish, such as turbot served with a classic beurre-blanc, deserve Chablis 1er Cru or a crisp Bordeaux Blanc. For the regal Dover sole on the bone, we recommend the finest white Burgundy you can afford.

Happily there is hope, too, for the teetotallers: kippers or kedgeree work wonderfully with a good pot of tea.

J Sheekey Wine Buyer, Richard Rotti

FISH AND SHELLFISH – BEST BETWEEN

Arbroath smokie	All year round
Atlantic prawn	All year round (weather permitting)
Brill	May to February
Brown shrimp	All year round
Caviar (farmed only)	All year round
Clam	All year round
Cockle	All year round
Cod cheek	October to June
Cod chitterling	January / February
Cod roe (smoked)	Fresh: February to April; frozen: all year round
Cod tongue	October to June
Cod	October to June
Dorset crab	All year round
Dover sole	May to February
Dublin Bay prawn / langoustine / scampi	All year round (weather permitting)
Gurnard	All year round
Haddock	October to June
Hake	October to June
Halibut	Wild: March to November; farmed: all year round
Herring roe	Fresh: February to April; frozen: all year round
Herring	July to April
John Dory	May to February
Kipper	All year round
Lemon sole	May to February
Mackerel	All year round
Monkfish	All year round
Mussel	September to April

Native lobster	May to end of September
Native oyster	September to April
Plaice	May to November
Pollack	October to June
Razor clam	All year round (weather permitting)
Red gurnard	All year round
Red mullet	All year round
Rock oyster	All year round
Salt cod	All year round
Sardine	July to April
Scallop	All year round (weather permitting)
Sea bass	August to April
Sea bream	August to April
Sea trout	April to 3rd week of August
Smoked anchovy	All year round
Smoked haddock	All year round
Smoked mackerel	All year round
Smoked salmon	All year round
Squid	May to February
Tiger prawn	All year round
Turbot	May to February
Whelk	All year round (weather permitting)
Whitebait	Fresh: June to August; frozen: all year round
Wild salmon	April to 3rd week of August
Winkle	All year round (weather permitting)

BIBLIOGRAPHY

Lindsey Bareham, *The Fish Store* (Michael Joseph, 2006)

Frances Bissell, *Sainsbury's Book of Food* (Websters International, 1989)

Larousse Gastronomique (Hamlyn, 2009)

Le Cordon Bleu, *Le Cordon Bleu Complete Cooking Techniques* (William Morrow, 1997)

Le Cordon Bleu, *Le Cordon Bleu Fish I* (BPC Publishing, 1971)

Le Cordon Bleu, *Le Cordon Bleu Fish II* (BPC Publishing, 1977)

Alan Davidson, *Oxford Companion to Food* (Oxford University Press, 2006)

Hugh Fearnley-Whittingstall and Nick Fisher, *The River Cottage Fish Book* (Bloomsbury, 2011)

Nick Fisher, *The River Cottage Handbook 6: Sea Fishing* (Bloomsbury, 2010)

Paul Greenberg, *The Fish on Your Plate* (Penguin, 2011)

Jane Grigson, *Fish Cookery* (Penguin, 1975)

Miles Irving, *The Forager Handbook* (Ebury, 2009)

C. J. Jackson and Barton Seaver, *Fish: Recipes from the Sea* (Phaidon, 2012)

Peter Jordan, *Field Guide to Edible Mushrooms of Britain and Europe* (New Holland, 2010)

Mark Kurlansky, *Cod: A Biography of the Fish that Changed the World* (Penguin, 1999)

Jekka McVicar, *Jekka's Complete Herb Book* (Kyle Cathie, 2009)

Anistatia Miller and Jared Brown, *Spirituous Journey: A History of Drink Book One* (Mixellany Ltd, 2009)

Anistatia Miller and Jared Brown, *Spirituous Journey: A History of Drink Book Two* (Mixellany Ltd, 2010)

Frederick Birmingham, *Esquire Drink Book* (Harper and Row, 1956)

Roger Phillips, *Mushrooms* (Macmillan, 2006)

Roger Phillips, *Wild Food* (Pan, 2007)

Roger Phillips and Martyn Rix, *Vegetables* (Pan, 2009)

Madame Prunier, *Madame Prunier's Fish Cookery Book* (Quadrille, 2011)

Rick Stein, *English Seafood Cookery* (Penguin, 2001)

Rick Stein, *Rick Stein's Seafood* (BBC Books, 2001)

ACKNOWLEDGEMENTS

We would like to thank the following individuals and companies for their help in producing this book. It has been a team effort. But first amongst equals must be Alvin Caudwell, Caprice Group Head of Sales & Marketing. This book would not be as it is without her assiduity and enthusiasm.

SPECIAL THANKS TO
Phil Usher, Caprice Group Pastry Chef
Timur Nidai, Sous Chef, J Sheekey
Mounia Ghannam, Caprice Group Marketing Assistant
Richard Kirkwood, Former Head Chef of J Sheekey & J Sheekey Oyster Bar

AT J SHEEKEY & J SHEEKEY OYSTER BAR
Marco Fazzina, General Manager
James Cornwall, Head Chef
John Andrews, Front of House Manager
Dominik Powroznik, Bar Manager
Front of House team
Kitchen team

AT CAPRICE HOLDINGS
Richard Caring, Chairman
Martin Dickinson, Group Executive Chef
Marketing team
Jamie Caring, Former Commercial Director
Richard Rotti, Group Wine Buyer
Xavier Landais, Group Bar Manager

SUPPLIERS
Allan Reeder Ltd
Andy Wilson and Terry Wenborn, Southbank Fresh Fish
Chapmans of Sevenoaks Ltd
Charlie Mash, Mash Purveyors Ltd
Clarence Court
David Haskell & Lincoln Barton, Southwest Fisheries Ltd
Guy Grieve, The Ethical Shellfish Company
I. Camisa & Son
Jesse Pattisson, Brown and Forrest Ltd
John Mower & Co Limited
Keltic Seafare (Scotland) Ltd
Kevin Bartlett, Top Catch Ltd
La Credenza Ltd
Matthew Stevens, Matthew Stevens & Son
Mike Dawson, West Mersea Oysters
Miles Irving, Forager
Millers Bespoke Bakery Ltd
Monica Linton, Brindisa Ltd
Paxton & Whitfield

Phil Britten, Solstice Limited
Portland Shellfish Ltd
Steve Downey, Chef Direct
The Fresh Olive Company
The Whitstable Oyster Company Ltd
Tony Booth, Tayshaw Ltd
Wild Harvest Ltd
Wright Bros. Limited

ALSO
Caroline Michel & Janelle Andrew (PFD)
Jared Brown (cocktails)
Trevor Pickett (pots & pans)
Nicola Stephenson and her team at Mission
Anouschka Menzies and her team at Bacchus
Chris Corbin and Jeremy King
Trevor Dolby and his team at Random House

INDEX

9 May 2012: St Martin's Court, London. The J Sheekey restaurant team, including General Manager Marco Fazzina, Front of House Manager John Andrews, Head Chef James Cornwall and "Baksh" the Doorman

ALLAN JENKINS, WRITER

Allan Jenkins is Editor of *The Observer Food Monthly*, working closely with some of Britain's country's best-loved writers and cooks, including Nigel Slater, Jeremy Lee and Simon Hopkinson. In the past year he has also reported from China, Denmark, India, Mexico, Sweden and Spain. He shares a biodynamic allotment and *The Observer*'s garden blog with *J Sheekey Fish* photographer Howard Sooley.

TIM HUGHES, CHEF

Tim Hughes is Chef Director of the Caprice group of restaurants, which counts J Sheekey, The Ivy and Scott's among its number. He first worked for the group at Le Caprice in 1990 under Mark Hix, and in 1998 was made Head Chef at the newly refurbished J Sheekey. He now oversees the group's restaurants and clubs in London and abroad. The lure of fish led him to his home on the south coast.

HOWARD SOOLEY, PHOTOGRAPHY

Howard Sooley was a successful fashion photographer for, among others, US and Japanese *Vogue* until he swapped shooting clothes and the catwalk for photographing portraits, gardens and food. His previous books include the ground-breaking *Derek Jarman's Garden* and the *Bocca di Lupo cookbook*. His work is held by the Tate and London's Garden Museum.